TABLE OF CONTENTS

A Handbook For
GRANDPARENTS

OVER 700 CREATIVE THINGS
TO DO AND MAKE WITH
YOUR GRANDCHILD

LYNN WILSON

◆ FriesenPress

Suite 300 - 990 Fort St
Victoria, BC, Canada, V8V 3K2
www.friesenpress.com

ISBN
978-1-4602-7795-9 (Hardcover)
978-1-4602-7796-6 (Paperback)
978-1-4602-7797-3 (eBook)

1. Family & Relationships, Parenting, Grandparenting

Distributed to the trade by The Ingram Book Company

Wilson has clearly understood the importance of developmentally appropriate experiences for young children. Her hands-on play based approach provides grandparents with an opportunity to build strong and loving relationships. I was especially pleased to see her focus on outdoor experiences which underscores our need to spend more time in nature.

PATRICIA CHORNEY RUBIN,
DIRECTOR, SCHOOL OF EARLY CHILDHOOD,
GEORGE BROWN COLLEGE

A Handbook for Grandparents is a wonderful resource full of developmentally appropriate play ideas that are fun and engaging for both children and adults. No expensive gadgets or screens are needed to support children's development, build relationships and promote mutual enjoyment. Wilson's book is pure refreshment for those who want to forge meaningful relationships with their grandchildren and support their children's parenting.

CONNIE WINDER,
FACULTY, GEORGE BROWN COLLEGE

This book is a wonderful collection of resources and I have used countless activities with my 3 granddaughters. I love how the resources move from simple to more complex ideas, encouraging new activities as our grandchildren grow!

PAM DOYLE,
GRANDMOTHER

I am so looking forward to becoming a grandma! Reading A Handbook for Grandparents helps me think about, and get ideas for, the values and experiences I hope to share with my grandchild. It takes effort NOT to become submerged in the commercial toy business, with all the 'bells and whistles' of expensive, short-term, mostly plastic toys, that focus on solitary play. The handbook helps us avoid those temptations with amazing activities: sharing time together, using natural materials, or objects that are inexpensive and around the house. This handbook is invaluable for grandparents...it will build memories that last a lifetime!

BARB PIMENTO,
GRANDMOTHER-TO-BE

EMMA AND HER GRANDPARENTS, AGE 5

"When Grandmothers speak,
the earth will be healed."

HOPI PROPHECY

A Handbook For GRANDPARENTS

OVER 700 CREATIVE THINGS

TO DO AND MAKE WITH

YOUR GRANDCHILD

LET'S GET
ORGANIZED

NATALIE'S NANA AND PAPA, AGE 5

YOU ARE A GRANDPARENT: CONGRATULATIONS!

FINDING A NAME FOR YOURSELF

Now what? First, you'll need a name. For new grandparents, what they will be called can generate much discussion and be great fun. Whether you are Granny, Gram, Nana, Grandmere, Nonna or Bubbe / Gramps, Grampa, Pop, Nonno, Grandpere or Opa, you will love this newest member of your family! Your children may have some input but children often find ways to name you that are non-traditional but "stick" because they become part of your family's story.

RARING TO GO

Because of longer life expectancies, more children have grandparents for longer periods of time than ever before. Young parents often look to their own parents for emotional, financial, and child care assistance and therefore we have a greater opportunity to provide intergenerational support to our children. Many grandparents are joyful at being able to love and care for their grandchildren without the worries and concerns that plagued them as parents! Free from the primary responsibility, we can offer a safe and nurturing environment where our grandchildren are loved unconditionally. No matter how you choose to approach grandparenting, your role is a special and a magical opportunity to support your grandchild in all facets of their lives.

Parents must also have realistic expectations about the amount of practical help some grandparents are willing and able to provide given their own plans for their retirement or their work commitments. Grandparents' involvement will vary significantly between families. The age and health of grandparents, age of the grandchildren, geographical locations, whether the grandparents are still working, and the relationship the grandparents have with their own child can all be factors. Some grandparents may live in multigenerational families, in which parents, grandparents and other relatives or friends live together. Other grandparents may live long distances from their grandchildren but the communication revolution has now made it possible for them to stay in touch. Some will become grandparents to step children. A growing phenomenon is grandparents raising their grandchildren in what are often referred to as skip-generation families when there is no parent present in the household. Grandchildren can move into this situation either through a legal process or a family agreement.

 ## FAMILY DYNAMICS

Family dynamics are always changing. Over time, there may well be many changes in your immediate and extended family. There are many challenging transitions that can affect families, and it's important to be respectful of each unique circumstance. A new baby, an adopted child, a move, a new school, illness, death, separation and divorce, another set of grandparents to build relationships with; these can all have a drastic effect on the members of any family. In many of these situations, your daughter or son will need your support as never before. Grandparents can provide the much needed stability during these demanding times.

 ## OPEN COMMUNICATION

As our children find partners who may be from different ethnic or religious backgrounds, grandparents will be exposed to various cultural influences and differing social conventions. This may influence the parents' beliefs, attitudes, and expectations to child rearing. Whatever the circumstances, successful relationships between all parties will depend on open communication. The parents will want to set in place the values that they think are most important as they create their own child-rearing philosophy and parenting style. At the core of our role with grandchildren is the support we can give to our children. Not leading, not telling, but following their lead; doing things as they would like them done and offering suggestions only when asked. While we have a special role and place in our grandchild's life, we must always remember that our children are the parents of the child and their wishes must take precedence. Criticism, of parenting or doing things "behind the backs" of the grandchild's parent(s) will only cause frustration, anger, and perhaps estrangement. You want to create healthy relationships with all of the players, including another set of grandparents, which reflects a non-confrontational approach that emphasizes that we are all in this together and we can solve whatever happens along the way. Open communication will be the key – insist on it!

 ## ABOUT THIS BOOK

This book is meant to give you lots of ideas for interacting with your grandchildren when they come to visit at your house. Many of the ideas also translate easily to your visits to their home as well. Numerous experiences in this book reinforce early learning skills but, most important, they are there to engender a meaningful connection between you and your grandchild. Play is how children learn. Knowledge and skills become meaningful when they are used during play as tools for learning – they are practiced and concepts become understood. Throughout this book, you will notice a multi-sensory approach with an emphasis on math and science as well as on language and literacy. The importance of engendering a love of books from the earliest age cannot be overestimated. Reading will be fundamental to your grandchild's understanding of the world around them. As you read through the book, you will find that in most areas the activities are divided into *Simple* and *More Complex Ideas*. This grouping of activities allows for children of varying ages and abilities to work at different levels on different activities. Each of your grandchildren is unique. Children have natural developmental differences as they grow so as you look through these activities, I hope that you will find experiences that will support your grandchild's individual development. None of these activities are static - the addition of an interesting piece of equipment may change a simple idea into a more complex one for older children – great adventures await!

You will also see web links throughout the book that will provide you with more ideas and opportunities to connect with your grandchild.

You are also about to see quotes from grandparents, parents and grandchildren. I hope these will deepen your understanding of the important part we all play in each other's lives! Many reflect a grandchild's deep connection to their grandparents; a person who never broke a promise, who always told the truth, someone who believed in them and kept their most precious secrets, a person who loved them unconditionally! Whether you are an almost grandparent, a first time grandparent, a seasoned pro or even a great grandparent, I hope this book will provide you with hours and hours of fun with your grandchild. Be their greatest audience! Enjoy!

"When I first became a grandparent my biggest emotion was pride in the way my daughter "rose to the occasion". I had always thought her to be a responsible and caring daughter, friend and colleague to others. Now I had to opportunity to see her as a mother... And it made me weep with pride." PAM, NANA

"Becoming a grandparent has been second only to becoming a mom! Being present in the delivery room was an over-whelming experience. (Also, a lot less painful!). I am truly in awe of my daughter as a mom, which is a bit unexpected. She is very confident and relaxed, something I don't think I was! Watching my grandson grow and develop has been so much fun and I look forward to the years and additional babies ahead." JULIE, GRANNY

"Having engaged grandparents in our daughter's life has had a tremendous impact on our family. When we are tired and don't pay enough attention to her magic, she sees wonder reflected in their eyes. When we are impatient and are too quick to get frustrated with her, they help us to marvel at her strength and tenacity again. When we worry that we are being too indulgent and become inflexible with her, they are there to cast the rules aside - to laugh and dance and eat ice cream with her. When we realize we could have loved her just a little bit better that day, we are relieved to know that they have loved her more than enough to make up the difference." ERIN, PARENT

YOU'RE READY BUT IS YOUR HOUSE READY?

1. YOUR ENTRANCE WAY: When children come for a visit or a sleep over, we all know they come with lots of bits and pieces! At the entrance to your home or apartment, you may want to organize hooks for coats and bins for hats and mitts (having these at the appropriate height is always a bonus). If an infant is coming, you will just need more space allocated to finding a home for everything that comes with a baby.

2. TABLE AND SHELVES: If you have the room, a small, a child-size table and chairs for doing activities is a great addition to your home. A small storage shelf will help keep you and your grandchild organized. If possible, more than one shelf helps you to sort and categorize materials. It will make it easy for them to help themselves, encouraging both independence, and a sense of order (infants and toddlers love to dump so you may want to consider that in your planning!). These shelves should be bolted to the wall.

3. A COZY CORNER: Creating a cozy corner where your grandchild keeps their special things when they come to visit makes accessing materials (and their favourite blanket) easy enough for them and for you.

4. STORAGE: Create some interesting storage containers that are fun and easy for the children to access. You and your grandchildren may want to personalize bins, one for each of your grandchildren.

a. If space is an issue, try sewing or purchasing some simple bags to hold items your grandchild is interested in and tie them to a hanger. You can also put items into a Ziploc bag so that you can see what's inside for quick access. You can get shower rings and some small clips and hang the Ziploc bags on the hanger as well (a quick and easy storage idea that keeps many of your resources in one place).

b. A shoe-bag hanger or a baby-diaper bag can also be a great place to put puppets, dolls or special items. It can be hung on the back of a door with a simple hook.

c. Small metal flower pots are great for storing items as are six-quart baskets, Tupperware containers, muffin tins, fishing tackle boxes or rinsed out egg cartons.

5. OUTFITTING YOUR HOME: There are many items that will help make the transition to Granny and Grampa's house less stressful. If possible, having a crib, a high chair and a car seat in your home, will make settling in easier for your grandchild and caregiving easier for you. While many of these items can be picked up at garage sales, eBay etc. don't forget other parents or grandparents whose children have outgrown these items. Always ensure that these are still safe and follow the current government guidelines.

6. TRAYS: Trays are a great way to contain children's masterpieces and make for a quick and easy clean up.

7. A SPECIAL SHOE BOX: Each time your grandchild visits put something new and interesting into a decorated shoe box. Place it near the front door and watch your grandchild head for it every time. What a great way to start the visit!

8. A TAKE HOME BAG: Create a special take home bag, sew it or have it made or convert another bag. Have the child personalize it with their name and some fabric paint. This can be the bag for loot or the back and forth bag to Granny and Grampa's house.

9. PLANNING AHEAD: A great way to get organized and create even more excitement about an upcoming visit with your older grandchildren is to call ahead and plan the menu. You can greet them, with aprons in hand and you and your grandchild can begin to make the feast!

"Grandparents have the pleasure of being able to share their true and complete selves with their grandchildren. My mom always said the only thing better than being a mom was being a grandmother and she was a pro at it. She was often inappropriate but that's what the kids loved about her. She let loose and could have a ton of fun just singing, dancing, playing games and acting silly. She could be as goofy and fun loving as she wanted and if things got out of hand, she would turn it over to me to handle!" KARYN, PARENT

MY GRANNY, SAMANTHA, AGE 3

You'll Need A Safe Environment

1. BE SAFE: The safety of your grandchild should always be your first priority but this issue really comes into play when your grandchild begins to move. So, try to imagine what it is like to be a little person - get down on your hands and knees and look at what you see. The first 24 inches belong to the child so having the items they need at their fingertips is essential. It is also an opportunity to see if there are things that could be harmful to your grandchild, such as plugs without covers, hanging wires or your favourite crystal vase. Little ones are capable of incredible investigative skills so move those priceless items up high. Toxic cleaning supplies should also be placed well out of their reach and locked away. Cupboards may need to have safety latches, and gates will help to prevent falls down stairs. Cords from telephones, computers, blinds or shades should be out of reach. Strings on clothing can also be a hazard on playgrounds. Be careful with necklaces or strings on pacifiers. You can put covers on sharp coffee table corners, and the entrance and exit doors should all be secure. Consider your plants as well, some common household plants are actually poisonous – Oleander, Poinsettia, Philodendron, Azalea and Amaryllis. If you have pets, they should be introduced slowly to the children.

2. CHOKING: Remember that choking is a serious issue for infants and toddlers - they put everything in their mouths. Anything that can fit inside a paper toilet roll can be a danger to them. Also avoid common choking hazards for young children such as peanuts, popcorn, raw vegetables, hard fruits or candies.

3. BACKGROUND INFORMATION: It is critical to know your grandchild's medical history as well as knowledge of any allergies or medications they might be taking and their blood type. Know what to give your grandchild if they become ill.

4. EMERGENCY INFORMATION: Whether your grandchild stays for a short time or a long time it is essential that you have at your fingertips all the necessary information should an emergency occur. The phone numbers of the parent's cell phones and work numbers; the name, phone number and address of the children's doctor; the child's health card or health card number; the number for the poison control centre and a well stocked first aid kit are essentials.

5. MONITORS: If your grandchild will be spending the night with you, you may want to invest in a monitor. There are many features that are available on these valuable aids – two cameras, motion, sound, temperature monitoring, audio allowing you to talk to your grandchild, night vision, the ability to take photos as well as playing lullabies for helping your grandchild get to sleep. Other options do not require a separate monitor; you access your camera directly through your Smartphone, tablet or computer. Lots of options to consider!

6. SAFE EQUIPMENT: Babies and children should be in car seats that meet the most current standards. Walkers with wheels are also not recommended as they pose a high risk as children propel themselves into hazardous situations. When riding tricycles or bicycles, skateboarding, rollerblading etc., your grandchildren should always wear a helmet and you should also role model by wearing one yourself. Wrist, elbow and knee pads may also be necessary.

7. ALARMS: Make sure you have installed smoke alarms and have a fire extinguisher on hand. You should also have carbon monoxide monitors.

8. SLEEPING: Infants under a year should be placed on their backs in their cribs to prevent Sudden Infant Death Syndrome. Cribs should have a firm mattress and to avoid suffocation, all soft objects or materials should be kept out of the crib. When your infant grandchild begins to want to climb over the crib you may want to invest in an inflatable mattress so that the child can sleep right on the floor if space is an issue. If a bed is available make sure it is placed against the wall and soft cushions are positioned on the other side.

9. HAND WASHING: Proper hand washing is recognized as one of the most important ways to stop the spread of illness. Encourage your grandchildren to wash

their hands with warm water and soap for as long as it takes to sing the Happy Birthday song. Introduce fun soaps with bright colours or interesting shapes and smells to keep them interested.

10. YOUR MEDICINES: All your medicines should be stored in child proof containers but more importantly they should be stored well away from your grandchildren and secured. Return any medications that you are not using to your local pharmacy for disposal. Avoid taking your medications or vitamins in front of your young grandchildren who often assume they are candy.

11. VACCINES: You should make sure that your vaccinations are up to date and that you have a flu shot if that is recommended. You need to stay healthy too!

12. OUTDOORS: Also check to make sure that your outdoor environment is safe. If you have a balcony, make sure that there are no stepping stools or chairs that a young child could climb on. Make sure that all of your windows have screens and locks. Look for overgrown plants that might scratch or injure your grandchild. Keep garbage cans and gardening equipment locked away. If you have a gate, make sure that it closes tightly to prevent your grandchild wandering away.

13. PETS: Be vigilant with young children especially around your pets. They need to understand how to properly care for these animals.

14. HOUSE RULES: Visits will go more smoothly if everyone knows what the house rules are. Decide on the things that are important to you — being gentle with the dog, we clean up our toys before bed, we help take out the garbage etc. Encourage their participation in the smooth running of the house as much as possible. Often children become over stimulated making it difficult for them to manage, these are times when you will need to be flexible and be prepared to listen to your grandchild's point of view. As you get to know your grandchild you will be able to anticipate what might be a problem in advance making for a more enjoyable time together. There will be many opportunities to encourage pro social behaviour in their attempts to manage in difficult and challenging situations. Children need guidelines and boundaries and consistency is important. Young children often become frustrated because they don't have the language to communicate their wants and needs. They can often be supported by redirecting them to something else that is eye catching or interesting and thereby avoiding an outburst. With older children, be clear in your expectations and make sure what you are asking is within their capabilities. Offer choices when that is possible; it helps them feel they have

some control over what is happening to them. Talk about their feelings when things don't go their way and never use any form of physical punishment. Use positive language – "I like the way you are helping to put the toys away", avoid loud voices and look for opportunities to catch them doing things right – celebrate this!

"Never in my life did I realize the importance and necessity of grandparents until the day my twin boys came home from the hospital. Within a few days of our independent approach ('we can do it ourselves'), we asked for help for the first time. Without blinking an eye, Grandma and Grandpa jumped into the mix with their sleeves rolled up and burping pads in place. Grandpa would show up to the house every morning and Grandma would help every evening. Even now that it has gotten easier to care for our tyrant toddlers, Grandma and Grandpa are an everyday part of their lives and we wouldn't want it any other way." AMY, PARENT

"My Grandma was the world's best hugger, her hugs seemed to be therapeutic and always warmed me up no matter how cold it was outside." ALI, GRANDDAUGHTER

MY GRANNY, KRISTEN, AGE 4

A WORD ABOUT TOYS

First, there is no requirement to rush out and purchase a truck load of toys. The toy industry may be a billion-dollar industry with an unlimited number of toys available for purchase, but many children can still find pleasure in simple materials, many of which are already in your home! If you do plan to buy some toys, you will find that they vary from simple and inexpensive to complex and expensive. Your choice of materials for both indoor and outdoor play will also vary based on the needs and interests of your grandchildren as well as your budget. Whatever toys you are considering, remember that playthings should support the children's physical, social, emotional and cognitive development and match their stage of development and their emerging skills. We must also be aware of the fact that the materials grandparents provide send powerful messages to our grandchildren. For example, toys that promote violence send messages that aggressive play is acceptable. Many grandparents will want to eliminate stereotypical and inaccurate models and look for playthings that support the development of their grandchild's imagination and stimulate enquiring minds.

 ## INFANTS AND TODDLERS

New babies are interested in faces, strong patterns and colours. Toys for this age group should include items that are durable, that they can hold, shake and put in their mouths – toys such as rattles, rings, textured balls, vinyl books, unbreakable mirrors, toys that squeak and soft toys that can be laundered because, sooner or later, everything will go into their mouths! Play mats or interesting quilts are an excellent choice since a good deal of their time is spent on their tummies. Mobiles hung in their cribs are engaging. Music is also important and lullabies can help sooth your grandchild. You can create your own playlists from a range of music (this is an opportunity to introduce music from a wide range of cultures). As babies grow, they begin to roll over and sit, crawl, pull themselves up and take those first tentative steps. Activity centres and activity bars for strollers are great fun at this stage. Teething rings, balls, household items that they will recognize, baby dolls, puppets,

and toys that move, squeak and pop up will also engage their interest. Once they are fully on their feet, they will enjoy pull and push toys, shape sorters, blocks, and nesting boxes. Toddlers will also enjoy playing house, looking at board books that show pictures of real objects, puzzles, blocks, dress-up clothes, construction toys with switches and knobs to turn, art and sensory experiences, plastic animals, little people, large beads that pop together, large peg boards and ride-ons.

PRESCHOOLERS AND SCHOOLAGERS

By the time your grandchildren reach preschool age, they will want to emulate the people they see in their lives and use the tools that their role models do: pots, pans, bowls, spatulas, briefcases, iPhones, tablets, and screwdrivers. There is no question that children prefer real objects to plastic replicas and frustration can arise when poor imitations are presented. Never forget that sand and water toys can provide hours of intense play. Art experiences begin to take shape at this stage. Your grandchild will also be interested in more complex books, musical instruments, hammering toys, CD and DVD players, computer games and collections that they generate. As they age your grandchildren may show an emerging interest in sports and this is an opportunity to provide the appropriate equipment. They are also ready for materials such as Duplo (under 3 years), Lego (3+ years), Bristle blocks, more complex puzzles, pegs and pegboards, beads for stringing, Lotto games, sewing cards and Unifix cubes. All are examples of manipulatives. These materials support the development of the concepts of size, shape, classification, sorting, grouping, seriation, patterning, and one-on-one correspondence which become more meaningful and relevant to children between six and eight years. Physically, the manipulation of these materials supports the development of both gross and fine motor skills and provides practice for eye-hand co-ordination and visual discrimination. When using these manipulatives, children are often interacting, learning how to co-operate with others and completing tasks successfully by trying out new ideas and taking risks.

"My grandchildren think I am old but cool, they often ask about the pioneer days that I grew up in. They are my greatest gift in life!" MONIQUE, GRAND-MERE

TOY SAFETY

Remember that safety is always our first priority. As grandparents, we would never want to introduce any materials that could be harmful if touched, eaten, chewed or could cause any type of adverse reaction. With safety always in mind, we should consider the durability of the toy, the kind of paint used, the size of detachable parts, the presence of sharp edges and the ease of cleaning and disinfecting - especially when babies are young and everything goes into their mouths. To get most toys clean, a good soap and water scrub and air drying should do the trick. Some toys may be machine-washed and others can be placed in the dishwasher. It is imperative that we always read the labels of new materials to ensure that they meet all regulations and safety standards. Look carefully for small-parts warnings such as a choking hazard and the recommended age for use. As stated earlier, use a toilet paper roll or choke tube to test the size of loose parts since this simulates the size and shape of a young child's throat. We must always be vigilant and check toys regularly for wear and tear that may make them unsafe. All toys are manufactured to comply with the rules and regulations of the *Hazardous Products Act*, administered by the *Health Canada Product Safety Bureau*. *The Canadian Toy Testing Council* is a non-profit organization that tests toys to help consumers make good toy purchases. Safety is always a first priority.

@ www.toy-testing.org/

@ www.hc-sc.gc.ca/cps-spc/advisories-avis/info-ind/requirements-conditions-eng.php

"My parents have been the single greatest support to me as a mom and to our family. Watching their interactions with my children and seeing how much their presence enriches my kids' lives is extraordinary. Their love and support for our family is irreplaceable, and we are tremendously fortunate to have them in our lives." MEGAN, PARENT

MY NANA, SARAH, AGE 4

GIFT GIVING

There are many opportunities throughout the year when gifts will be given. Finding ways to give meaningful gifts is an opportunity to engender a growing sense of community and the needs of others in your grandchildren. It is always best to run your gift ideas past your grandchildren's parents to ensure that they feel your gift is appropriate and that they haven't had the same idea!

1. RESP: University tuition is at an all time high and many young men and women are deciding to live away from home to go to college or university or participate in apprenticeship programs. It may be hard to envision that happening when you are celebrating the birth of your first grandchild but it may be one of the most meaningful gifts you could ever give to both your grandchild and their parents. Given that the government offers incentives to create RESP's, this is a really good longer term choice. You may make a once a year contribution on special occasions or holidays but overtime even the smallest donation will make a difference. Another advantage is that these funds can only be used for educational purposes. There is a family plan option that even if one grandchild decides not to further their education, other siblings can enjoy the benefits.

2. SAVINGS ACCOUNT: Another option is to set up a savings account helping young children to understand the need to save when they want to purchase something special for themselves or someone else. Select an account that caters to children and carries no fees. They might have a piggy bank at home and once a month you make a trip with them to the bank. It is also an opportunity to discuss a ratio between spending and saving. Some families also focus on charity giving and so a percentage of the funds go to supporting a community or international organization.

3. ONLINE ACCOUNTS: Yet another option which allows flexibility is to open an online account. You are able to deposit funds right from home. This may be an opportunity to discuss investing and money management with older children.

4. HERITAGE CHEST: You may begin this heritage chest on the day your grand-child is born. You might save the newspaper that was printed on that day, you might record the weather, your version of their delivery and this can be an ongoing project for many years. It may be given on a special occasion, a 16th birthday or as a wedding gift.

5. BOOKS: There is no greater gift than generating excitement about a new book!

6. AUDIO BOOKS: A gift certificate to find books they would like to listen to might be a fun idea.

7. LETTER PRESENT: Using heavy tag board or thin wood cut into the shape of the first initial of your grandchild's name, cover it with pictures of your grandchild then varnish over top and add a wall clip on the back for easy hanging.

8. PLANT SOMETHING SPECIAL: Plant a rose bush or a favourite tree for each grandchild. Perhaps you can find a plant that has the same name as your grandchild – Iris, Dahlia, Rosemary, Daisy etc.

9. PERSONALIZED GIFTS: You may want to personalize a beach towel, a snuggle blanket or any other items of interest. This is particularly helpful if you have more than one grandchild. Use fabric crayons and create a special pillow case. You might give them a piece of their art work in a wonderful frame. Cookies or cakes with their names or initials on them – imagine!!

10. EDIBLE GIFT: If you know your grandchild's favourite treat is Rice Krispie Squares for example, you might put together in an interesting box all the materials to make the squares.

11. SPECIAL GIFTS: Consider giving a gift certificate for a hairdresser, or paying for skating lessons, gymnastics classes, a new bike or ice skates etc. There may be times when grandparents are in a better financial situation than their children and these gifts may make a great difference.

"One of my fondest memories of my grandfather is him helping me to skate. He was an incredible athlete and he so enjoyed our time together. We went from him teaching me to skate to now playing shinny hockey on Saturday mornings with him and his friends!" LIAM, GRANDSON

12. PRACTICAL GIFTS: You might purchase a tool box with child size hammers, screwdrivers, measuring tape etc. for your granddaughter to encourage some important life skills or a bag filled with gardening tools for a budding naturalist.

13. MEMBERSHIPS: Many organizations such museums, art galleries etc. have yearly family memberships and are great family gifts.

14. BACK TO SCHOOL BACKPACK: You may want to purchase a new backpack for the start of the school year and fill it with all kinds of interesting and fun supplies. At another time when you are heading off on an adventure together you may fill it with things that will contribute to the fun – a trip to the beach – sunscreen, bug spray, a new fancy towel, sun hat etc.

15. COUPONS: You might give your grandchildren "coupons" that they can cash in – for example, "Grampa and I will take you to a drive-in movie", "One game of mini golf", "We will buy you one back-to-school outfit".

"Every year when it's time to begin thinking of going back to school, my granddaughter and I go shopping to buy her first day of school outfit. We have been doing this for many years and it has become one of the most enjoyable traditions that I have with my granddaughter. We also splurge on a delicious lunch as well!" ADITA, DAADEE

16. GIFTS FOR OTHERS: A gift that is compassionate and reflects concern for others can have a lifelong impact. Perhaps you and your grandchild could search out

charities that you would like to support and make a donation. You may want to use a gift catalogue from a well known charity and purchase items through them. As children get older and more aware of worldwide issues, helping them to feel as if they can have a positive impact is so critical. Craig Keilburger and his organization *Free The Children* is a wonderful example of a 12 year old boy on a mission and may well resonate with your growing grandchildren.

17. BIRTHDAYS: Some families are encouraging children instead of bringing a birthday present to make a donation to a local charity. Others ask for a small token but a larger donation be made in the birthday child's name.

18. EVENTS: If you know that your older grandchild loves a certain rock star, a pair of tickets for her and her best friend would be an exciting gift to give. Just make sure you have permission from her parents first!

19. LET'S GET OUTSIDE: With growing issues about obesity and children's lack of connection to nature, perhaps encouraging an outdoor hobby by purchasing equipment to play hockey, tennis, surfing, or hiking may be the start of a lifelong passion.

"Grandparents are the ones who sneak you treats, say yes when your parents say no and hug you until you can't breathe." KRISTY, GRANDDAUGHTER

MY NANNY AND PA, ASHLEY, AGE 4

TRANSITIONS

Young children are often reluctant to move to a new activity or event when they are engrossed in what they are doing. Big and little people's understanding of the concept of time is very different. Some children manage change easily while others need more time. It is important to give children a "heads up" when a transition will soon be taking place using age appropriate language that is clear and outlines the process in short simple steps. We do know that the more your grandchild can predict and participate in the happenings throughout the day, the less likely you will see challenging behaviour. Observe your grandchild carefully and anticipate when their energy is lagging. Overall it is important to remain positive.

1. PLAN AHEAD: Make sure you explain clearly what you will be doing in language that is age appropriate. "We are going to play one more hand of cards then we need to get in the car to go food shopping".

2. CHOICE: Children need a sense that they have some control over their environment and the things that are happening to them. "We can finish our card game or we can play one round of Connect 4 before we leave for shopping. What would you like to do"?

3. 5 MINUTE WARNING: Some children respond well to a timed warning that gives them the opportunity to work through the transition.

4. BEAT THE CLOCK: Sometimes a visual timer or a stop watch can help through the process or a sand hour glass that the child can turn over themself.

5. TIDY UP: Sometimes just a few sentences can make a difference, for example if you say, "Do you want to tidy up?" chances are they will just say NO! Try instead "Do you want to pick up the red toys or the green toys first? I will help you".

6. SING: These transitions can be much more fun if you sing your way through it – "It's Time To Tidy Up" "This Is The Way We Brush Our Teeth" or when they are being really silly sing: "Shake, shake, shake your sillies out, Shake shakes your sillies out, Shake, shake, shake your sillies out and wiggle your waggles away". You can make up your own words to just about any nursery rhyme.

7. TRANSITION TOY: Sometimes bringing out a favourite toy and using that to encourage your child to snuggle up with an old friend on your way to food shopping will ease the transition.

8. GIVE THEM A JOB: Children tend to be much more cooperative when they feel they are part of the process. "We need to feed the dog before we go shopping, can you help me with that"?

9. SUPERHERO: When moving on to the next part of the day is critical you might help your grandchild by tucking a towel or scarf into their shirt and asking them to fly with you to the front door.

"My grandson has Autism and we have found over time that routines are so important. The structure helps him to anticipate what will happen next. We also focus on breaking down the "what comes next" steps into small chunks. We want to do everything we can to help him be successful and to enhance his self esteem." KAREEM, JEDDI

"The trust of a grandchild is a gift. It ignites the child in you." ERIC, GRAMPS

MY NANA, MADDEN, AGE 4

BATH TUB FUN

There are some children who can't wait to get into the tub and others who are really hesitant. For those who are a bit worried, you may want to fill the tub before they come into the bathroom. For some children the sound of the running water is just too scary! You can also put some of these ideas you see below into the water to entice even the most reluctant grandchild. Tips – make sure you run the cold water first before you add the hot and never leave your grandchild alone in the bathroom!

Simple Ideas

1. MESSY TIME: The bath is a perfect place to carry out some really messy activities and all the mess just washes down the drain at the end of the play!

2. SOAPS: Use a variety of soaps in water and see which one soaps up the fastest or which soap smells the best? Use a fizzy water "bomb" – many of these are available with a variety of fragrances, flower petals and are very dramatic.

3. MAKING WAVES: Place large combs in the tub or sink for your grandchildren to make waves.

4. BOOKS IN THE TUB: Plastic books meant for water are available.

5. PUPPETS: Make bath puppets by sewing two wash cloths together and decorating.

6. SPRINKLERS: Punch holes in old yogurt containers etc. for a shower affect.

7. SING WATER SONGS: "This is the way we wash our hair, wash our hair, wash our hair. This is the way we wash our hair so early in the morning" (adjust for the time of day).

8. PAINT THE WALLS: Put shaving cream and food colouring into muffin tins along with a brush. Paint the tub and the walls. It all washes away.

9. FANCY HAIR: Create shampoo highlights by sculpting shampooed hair into funny shapes – use a plastic mirror to show off the results. You may also want to take some photos!

10. FISH: You can find craft foam in most craft stores and from this you can create your own fish for the tub.

11. WATER FLUTES: Water flutes can be filled with different amounts of water and they create different sounds. They also come with a waterproof music sheet.

12. BUBBLE MACHINE: There are bubble machines that you can purchase that are a fun addition to tub time!

13. TAP, TAP, TAP: Try tapping a variety of objects underwater – i.e. Metal spoons, toy cars, cups (water carries sound better than air).

More complex Ideas

1. PING PONG: Add ping pong balls to the water. For older children print the letters of their name with magic marker on the balls.

2. PIPES AND TUBES: A simple trip to Canadian Tire and you can find pipes and tubes that can transform the bath experience.

3. UNDERWATER VIEWER: Make a viewer with a paper cup with the bottom cut out, some clear plastic wrap and a rubber band or make a larger one using a milk carton.

4. COLOURING THE WATER: Reinforce colour concepts by adding food colouring to the water and corresponding toys and containers in that colour.

5. FLASHLIGHTS: Submersible flashlights are available. Turn out the lights!

6. UNDER WATER: Glow sticks and other submersible lights add a whole new experience to tub time.

7. SPONGES: Sponges cut into a variety of shapes – circles, squares etc. Thick ones, thin ones, the more the merrier.

 ## FURTHER READING:

Round Is A Mooncake by Lin
A Circle Here, A Square There by Diehl
Black On White by Hoban
Flip A Shape: Play! By Sami

8. ICE: Place ice cubes in the bath tub. For even more fun, create ice sculptures by placing water into a variety of plastic containers in different sizes and hiding

small toys inside each. As the ice melts in the tub, the toy becomes more accessible. Add food colouring for even more interesting blocks of ice! A great idea for a hot day!

9. ICY HANDS: Put water into plastic gloves and put them into the freezer. Put these frozen hands into the tub after removing the plastic. You can add food colouring for a variety of colours.

10. BOATS: Provide materials for making boats such as cut up egg cartons, toothpicks, straws, markers, construction paper and glue.

11. RINSING HAIR: One splash will be cold water, which one will it be?

"I have a memory of my Grandma brushing out my knotted hair after a bath and she told me instead of saying "ouch" to meow like a cat. I began meowing and she would meow right back... and then I started hissing at her, which eventually turned into fits of laughter." ALEXANDRA, GRANDDAUGHTER

"My memories of my Grandma always start with a smell. Ingrained in my head is my Grandma's perfume, her roast beef dinner, her laundry and her face powder. There are times now when I get a slight smell and it instantly takes me back to a place of happiness, laughter and security. I spent my time watching her, I was the little kid on the chair beside her when she cooked, I was the little kid who stood closely beside her when she hung the laundry, I was the little kid who sat on the side of the tub when she pinned her hair, I was the little kid who held the glass when she poured a drink, I was the little kid always close by watching. The adult me would give anything to go back and be that little kid, sitting at her feet, wishing I could keep watching." KELLY, GRANDDAUGHTER

12. FUN PHOTOS: If you have an underwater camera, you may want to record some of the children's bath tub antics.

13. ALPHABET ICE CUBES: Place plastic letters of your grandchild's name in ice cube trays and freeze them. Pop them into the tub and try to chase the letters of your grandchild's name.

14. COLOUR TABLETS: Rather than using food colouring you may want to try Color My Bath H2O La La Color Changing Bath Tablets. They are scent free, won't stain and are safe for use. 300 tablets per container so lots of colourful fun.

MY PAPA, ZACK, AGE 3

COOL DOWN, NIGHTY NIGHT/SLEEP OVERS

There may be times when getting children to nap or settle for the night may be difficult. Your grandchild might be hungry, over tired, over stimulated or they may even be experiencing separation anxiety, missing their parents and perhaps other siblings. An infant's sleep environment should include a firm mattress without any soft objects and they should be laid to rest on their back. With older children, for a smoother transition, give them lots of warning that bed time is fast approaching. When you have more than one grandchild you may want to consider having them sleep over one at a time. It gives you real one on one time with each grandchild.

1. ROUTINE: Try to keep to your grandchild's normal routine as much as possible. Make sure that naps that are taken during the day happen earlier rather than later so that they will be sleepy by bedtime. A busy afternoon at the playground will also help with bedtime. The process of settling down to sleep will be more effective if your grandchildren can anticipate a routine.

2. BLANKIE: You may want to shop together for a perfect comfort toy or blanket to help your grandchild settle when they come for a sleep over.

3. TIME TO GO TO SLEEP/TIME TO GET UP: Young children often have different ideas of what a sleep-in means. For really early risers there is a clock available that has a cloud on it when the child is to be sleeping and a sun that flips up into place at the assigned time when it is time to get up – this may be a useful investment!

4. MUSIC: A change in tempo with calming music is helpful in the cool down process.

5. WINDING DOWN GAME: Pick an activity or game that allows for some quiet time before bed.

6. TIP TOE: Playing a game of tip toeing around the house is a good way to slow them down. "Let's tip toe to the tub".

7. NIGHTY NIGHT: When it is time for bed you may want to help your grandchild put their toys to bed, sing the toys a good night song then proceed with your routine.

8. VISUALS: Create a story board with the pictorial steps for getting ready for bed. This may be particularly helpful for children with special needs.

9. BOOKS: Many grandchildren remember the times when they were snuggled in bed with their grandparent reading them a book before sleep. Sometimes that means many books as opposed to just one! Try to avoid books that are scary at this time of day!

10. BACK RUBS: Many children enjoy a back rub as they drift off. Light finger touches on the back may work wonders.

11. SINGING: One of my children's fondest memory is of their grandmother singing them to sleep with "You Are My Sunshine".

12. AUDIO BOOKS: Sometimes using audio books in bed is an interesting alternative and your grandchild may well close their eyes while listening.

13. CEILINGS: If your grandchild has the luxury of a room of their own, glow in the dark stickers can be used to create magnificent constellations on the ceiling.

14. FRIENDS: As children get older, they may have a hard time parting with friends for the weekend. One option might be to let them bring a friend for the sleepover! You will be the best grandparents ever!!

EXTENDED VISITS

If your children are going away for an extended period of time, it is important to prepare as much as possible in advance. Understand that separation anxiety can occur in children of all ages and while it can be difficult for everyone, it demonstrates that healthy attachments have been formed. Gregarious children may make the transition without a backward look. Children who find it hard to adapt to new things may have the occasional tearful episode when they abruptly remember where they are – or rather, where they are not. For some when the novelty of being at Granny and Grampa's place wears off, they start to miss the way things used to be. This is often evident during sleep routines and during meal times. Above all you will need to be patient and in tune with your grandchild's abilities and rhythms. Promptness is the single most important factor in stopping crying and we know that responding to a young child's cries immediately reduces the number of incidents. Conversely, ignoring a baby's cries may increase crying. You cannot spoil a baby! To ease the transition with older children, you might talk to your grandchild about the plans for the day so that they can anticipate what is to come. Plan events that will captivate your grandchild!

1. LIPSTICK KISSES: As mom says goodbye, have her leave a lipstick kiss on your grandchild's hand as a reminder of how much she loves her.

2. MOM'S PERFUME: Mom might spray some of her perfume on her child's blankie as a comfort at sleep time.

3. COMFORT TOYS: You might have a basket of soft comfort toys to help with the sleep routine.

4. MY MOM/DAD'S BOOK: It may be comforting for your grandchildren to hear their voices on tape or on a phone reading one of their child's favourite stories. There are also books available where parents can record their own voices.

5. SLEEP MUSIC: Parents might like to tape themselves singing their child's favourite sleep song.

6. FLASHLIGHTS: Small child size flashlights are available and this is great fun for a grandchild who might be a little wary about sleeping at Granny or Grampa's house.

7. NIGHTLIGHT: If you know your grandchild worries about the dark, there are many colourful and imaginative nightlights for purchase.

8. PILLOW TIME: You might have a photo of the family scanned onto a pillowcase or blanket.

9. PHOTO ALBUM: Your children could prepare a small photo album filled with family photos. This might come in handy at bedtime.

10. FACETIME: At bedtime you might FaceTime to say goodnight. Decide if this will help or make things more difficult since bedtime is when young children often miss their families the most. You can also text or email during the day.

11. DRAWINGS: Encourage your grandchild to create drawings for their parents expressing their feelings about the separation.

"My Grandmother was an oasis of calm in the turmoil of my youth." DEE, GRANDAUGHTER

"Being a grandparent has allowed me to experience a different kind of love that is like no other. It is a love that is completely unfettered and pure! I am grateful for that." JILL, GRANNY JILL

 FURTHER READING:

Dr. Seuss's Sleep Book by Dr. Seuss
Where Do Diggers Sleep At Night by Caplan Sayres
Feet Go To Sleep by Bottner
Go To Sleep Maddie by Wright
Sheep Go To Sleep by Shaw
Goodnight Moon by Wise Brown
Just Go To Bed by Mayer

MY GRANDMA, JJ, AGE 5

AROUND THE
HOUSE

INDOOR FUN

1. TIDY UP: Young children should be encouraged to put their toys in a basket or put their books on a shelf. These simple tasks are the beginning of important life skills.

2. TUPPERWARE: Simple plastic containers with their lids, in a variety of shapes, will provide hours of fun for little ones. This experience reinforces fine motor skills, one to one correspondence, and spatial relationships. When interest begins to wane, add small objects that your grandchildren can place inside the containers. Encourage them to shake and rattle their containers. Emptying things is a favourite activity for little people.

3. POTS AND PANS: Create your own band with a variety of pots and pans and their lids and lots of different sound makers – spoons, spatulas, flippers etc.

4. WORKING TOGETHER: There are many child size tools that are now on the market that allow your grandchild to help more effectively around the house. Small mops, brooms, dust pans, spray bottles, garden tools are now all available and just right for little hands.

5. DUSTING: A feather duster will provide lots of opportunities to shine up the house.

6. WINDOWS: Low windows can be sprayed with vinegar and water for a quick clean up with some paper towels or newspaper.

7. WASHING DISHES: If you have a sturdy stepping stool – presto – you have a dishwasher! Children love water and bubbles so let them help with the clean up. A plastic apron may help keep them dry!

8. FORTS: Gather lots of blankets, towels, old sheets, and pillows big and small to make a fort in the living room or over the clothes line outside. Big squeezy clips can help keep the fort together. Make sure you save large cardboard boxes from new appliances – they make perfect forts!

9. PETS: If you have a pet in your home, this is a great opportunity to teach your grandchild all the things that are necessary to care for and love a pet. Watch little ones carefully.

"Saying my Grandma was an animal lover is a bit of an understatement. She was one with the animals! She sang about them, she communicated with them, she taught us about them, she loved them." ALI, GRANDDAUGHTER

"Some of my fondest memories of my Granny and Grampa were of events in their house. Papa's chair was off limits for the kids and whenever we had family gatherings. Granny always made sure the freezer was stocked with Popsicles for all of us kids." MIKE W., GRANDSON.

10. FISH: If you have the space and the inclination, you might set up an aquarium together or perhaps a smaller version – a fish bowl.

More complex Ideas

1. WHAT'S OUTSIDE MY WINDOW: Sometimes some of the most interesting things happen in the outdoors when children are inside looking out. If you are lucky and have a window ledge that the children can sit on, add paper and pencils and a clipboard, markers, notebooks, and encourage the children to draw or write

about what they see. If you add "stick on" hummingbird feeders to the window or hang a piece of beef suet in an onion bag at a nearby tree, magic can happen!

2. CUTLERY: **S**ort all the spoons and forks into the right compartment.

3. SET THE TABLE: A good one to one correspondence activity – have your grandchild help you set the table for a meal. They might create a lovely decoration for the centre of the table using flowers from the garden.

4. VACUUMING: Many models are lightweight and easy to use and may be an activity that your grandchild would enjoy.

5. LAUNDRY: Your grandchildren will use categorizing, counting, and matching skills as they sort items such a socks into pairs while helping you with the laundry. Folding facecloths and hand towels is also lending a helping hand.

6. PLANTS: Watering plants both inside and outside the house provides opportunities to learn more about plants.

7. SEWING: Teach your grandchild how to sew on a button. More elaborate sewing projects might be undertaken as your grandchildren age. Simple ideas such as little sleeping bags for their stuffed animals or an apron for them to wear during kitchen fun are easy to sew.

8. EXERCISE: Lots of fun can be had when you exercise together. Large exercise balls can be a real workout. Skip together!

9. SPA DAY: There may be a perfect time when everyone needs to have a manicure or new colours on their toes.

10. FIRST AID: Many older children would benefit from First Aid Training. This is a life skill that will give children confidence when dealing with a first aid issue for themselves or their friends. This is particularly relevant if your grandchild is often alone at home after school until their parents return from work.

11. HOBBIES: This may be an opportunity to engage your grandchild in your interests. They might help you count coins if you are a coin collector, learn to play the guitar if you do, there are so many possibilities. Maybe you will learn about something new together!

FURTHER READING:

Kids To The Rescue: First Aid Techniques For Kids by Boellts
My Very First First Aid Book: A Simple Guide To
First Aid For Younger Children by Lees
First Aid by Canizares
The Kids Guide To First Aid: All About Bruises, Burns, Stings, Sprains And
Other Ouches by Buhler

"Grandparents are your role models, your guidance and the star in the sky to remind you that you are never alone." KRISTY, GRANDDAUGHTER

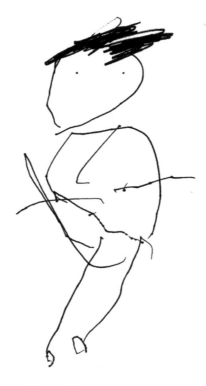

MY BUBBE, AIDEN, AGE 3

FUN IN THE KITCHEN

Children learn best when they are actively involved so the kitchen is a perfect environment. When interested and all of their senses are engaged children thrive, so provide opportunities for listening, touching, tasting, smelling, and feeling. We also know that children who help to prepare meals are more likely to try new foods. We encourage healthy eating habits, that we hope will last until adulthood, when we explore the textures, colours, and tastes of our foods without pressuring the children. Introducing new foods alongside one of their favourites is a good strategy. Cooking also allows them to feel a sense of pride and accomplishment when they are able to prepare and share what they have made. Making food together is the beginning of traditions that will be carried from generation to generation. We live in a culturally rich environment so we can learn about foods from other countries and experiment together!

The kitchen is an incredible place to learn life skills! With gentle guidance little hands are more than capable of stirring, whisking, rolling, measuring, tossing, sprinkling, kneading, spreading, pouring, and squeezing. Give them lots of opportunities to do this by providing small sizes and lightweight unbreakable materials which support the development of eye hand co-ordination and both gross and fine motor skills. There will be times when you will need to be patient but above all, be prepared for a mess! The kitchen is also a perfect place to learn new words and expand on a child's vocabulary. Early math, science and literacy skills are clearly at work when they count the number of eggs they need, measure, pour, and follow recipe instructions. Great fun awaits!

 ## KITCHEN SAFETY TIPS:

a. Be aware of any food sensitivities or allergies that your grandchild might have.

b. For little ones, to minimize food spills, place a piece of plastic under the highchair or purchase a plastic shower curtain or table cloth from the dollar store. Keep wipes handy!

c. Encourage your grandchild to wash their hands with soap and water before, during, and after your cooking experience, especially when touching raw meat, poultry, eggs or fish products. Make sure their hands are dry as wet hands can cause slips.

d. Tie back long hair, roll up sleeves, avoid baggy clothes that could get caught and wear an apron.

e. Clear away any materials at your workstation that might be dangerous to your grandchild. Watch for dangling electrical cords.

f. Use clean utensils and cutting boards should be designated for specific foods such as meat, fish, eggs etc.

g. This is an opportunity to discuss how to handle food to keep it from spoiling and how to store food properly.

h. Provide a sturdy step stool when needed or provide all of the items needed at a child size table.

i. The children should always have adult supervision whenever they are in the kitchen, particularly when dealing with hot liquids, the stove or sharp knives.

j. Proper use of the stove is essential, handles on pots should point to the back of the stove and hot foods should be kept away from the edges of counters or tables.

k. Consider silicone handled utensils because they do not transfer heat.

l. Wipe up spills as you go and encourage your grandchild to help with the kitchen clean up!

"My grandmother's cooking and baking stand out for me! Her Lemon Snow, Strawberries and Custard tasted like heaven." KARYN, PARENT

Simple Ideas

1. GETTING READY: You will save time and keep your little ones interested if you have your counters cleared off and all the ingredients and materials that you will need ready to go.

2. SPECIAL GEAR: Help them get into the mood for cooking by providing a chef's hat, an apron and child size items such as spoons, child friendly plastic knives, a bigger plastic bowl than needed to help contain energetic stirring etc.

3. TOUCHIE, FEELIE: Infants will enjoy the sensations of touch, smell and taste when they explore an orange, a lemon, a grapefruit etc. Put it right in their laps! Babies can sit in their seats on the counter, if it's safe; while they watch you prepare their food. Talk about what you are doing and label the fruits and vegetables. Sing whenever you can!

4. FROM THE HIGHCHAIR: Having your grandchild in the kitchen provides many opportunities for tasting and also for helping. Place items on the tray and talk about them, experiment with "hot" and "cold" items etc. You can also give them their own bowl and spoon and items inside to stir.

5. PLAY SETS: There are sets that mimic cooking and baking tools that are just right for little hands.

6. QUICK AND EASY: As young children have a limited attention span you may want to engage in experiences that give you quick results by preparing together scrambling eggs, wraps, juicing, smoothies, salads etc.

7. RINSE AWAY: With a sturdy stool, your grandchild could be in charge of washing fruits and vegetables.

8. TEAR IT UP: Toddlers can be given the task of tearing up lettuce or spinach for the salad.

9. SPICE IT UP: Shaking on spices at the end of the preparation is perfect for the final touches – adding cinnamon, nutmeg, oregano etc. Be careful that the spices won't hurt their eyes if they touch them with their fingers.

10. SHAKE IT UP: Let your grandchild shake up a milk drink in a tight container.

11. SNAP: Give your grandchild green beans to snap.

12. DIP IT: Vegetables and fruit always taste better if you can dip them into something interesting – try salsa, guacamole, yogurt etc.

13. SPREADING: Using a food spreader, give your grandchild soft spreads or peanut butter (if not allergic) to put on top of a sturdy cracker.

14. ANTS ON A LOG: Use a stick of celery and have them spread peanut butter on the inside or cream cheese and add raisins on top!

15. COLOUR DAY: Provide vegetables and fruits that are just one colour – strawberries, radishes, tomatoes, red peppers, raspberries etc.

16. CUT AND SNIP AWAY: With a plastic serrated child friendly knife, young children can cut up strawberries, cooked carrots, cucumbers etc. They can also nibble along the way! For little hands, try giving them a pair of blunt scissors to cut green onions, basil, parsley, or dried fruit such as apricots.

17. CRUSHING: Using a Ziploc bag, place items such as graham crackers into the bag and ask your little one to crush and smash away. You can also use a rolling pin. Use the crumbs for a pie crust.

18. MASH IT UP: Let your grandchild have a go at mashing potatoes!

19. COOKIES: Thumb print cookies are a quick and easy personalized experience.

20. COOKIE CUTTERS: Let your grandchild roll out the dough and use different cookie cutters to make some interesting treats. Try the cutters on cheese, veggies and bread.

21. FRUIT KABOBS: Using fruit that is easy to skewer, cut melons and pineapples, grapes etc. and thread them onto wooden skewers for a tasty and healthy treat. They may enjoy dipping their fruit into yogurt.

"My grandparents were my safe haven. A place I could go with no judgement, no reservation, no attitude, just love and acceptance - and a peanut butter sandwich...always - even when she was 94 and I was in my 50's." TERRY, GRANDSON

22. FOIL WRAP: Give your grandchild pieces of foil and ask them to wrap up potatoes for baking.

23. BANANA FUN: You can precut pieces of banana and score the skin so that your grandchild can peel the skin away. Then they can roll the banana in a bowl of cereal!

24. COATINGS: When you need something coated, put your meat inside a Ziploc bag and have your grandchild pour in the Panko or bread crumbs. Seal tightly and shake away.

25. SQUISHY SNACKS: You need a third of a banana, a large spoonful of peanut butter and a small Ziploc bag. Put all the ingredients in the bag and make sure it is sealed tightly. Let your grandchild squish away until the ingredients are all mixed. Push all the ingredients to one corner of the bag, snip off the end of the bag with scissors and squeeze the mixture onto bread or crackers.

26. SHAKING APPLE SLICES: Shake up plain apple slices by putting several into a Ziploc bag and letting your grandchild sprinkle on cinnamon. Seal up and shake away.

27. SANDWICHES: Make open face sandwiches with faces – raisins for eyes, a piece of carrot for a nose, a slice of radish for the mouth and sprouts for hair. All kinds of options await.

28. SNACK NECKLACES: Using a string for a necklace or a licorice string, you can loop on pretzels, Cheerios etc. and eat away.

29. PRETZELS: Pretzels are often a favourite snack but they are more delicious dipped in chocolate!

30. HOME MADE PRETZELS: Using refrigerated biscuit dough, roll it out and divide it into two pieces. Twist the pieces together into the shape of a pretzel. You can sprinkle on all kinds of goodies then bake!

31. SILLY SUPPER: Have a silly supper – backwards supper - with dessert first.

32. JOBS IN THE KITCHEN: Even young children can begin the process of cleaning up the kitchen, provide interesting sponges to clean the counters, help them put

the dishes away and cutlery into the right slots, match lids with their containers, sweep the floor etc.

33. BENTO BOXES: For picky eaters who don't want their foods touching each other or for those who want to view their food carefully before they eat it, Bento Boxes or plastic ware that has separate sections are perfect! It also helps to save on packaging.

"I spent most of my summers during grade school up north with my grandma and grandpa. They both loved to have me and my sister up and we were also very lucky to bring up our friends on many occasions. She was also a great baker and loved cooking for her family during many holidays spent up north." MIKE, GRANDSON

More complex Ideas

1. LIST MAKING: When your older grandchild is coming over, you may want to ask them to create two lists — one of all the things they never want to eat at your house and the other list is full of their favourite things.

2. GROCERY SHOPPING: Everyday events such as grocery shopping are a great opportunity for children to learn about the world around them. You might go to the store just for the ingredients for your latest project together. Let your grandchild help to pick out what is needed from your list and unpack all the goodies when you get back home. Even young babies will delight in the colours and sounds of a supermarket.

3. SHOPPING TOGETHER: When shopping with older children it is a great opportunity to look at the labels of the foods they are choosing. Which things are high in sugar or salt and low on nutrition? They are now on the way to making healthy choices.

4. MARKETS: Visit interesting markets, perhaps ones that reflect cultures other than your own. Sort your purchases when you get home, all the fruits on this side of the counter and the vegetables over here!

5. PICK YOUR OWN: Traveling to a "pick your own" farm is a great way to help children understand where their food comes from.

6. PRESERVING: Preserving pickles or making jam are fun ways to work and play together. Check out the different ways that food can be preserved – for example, apricots – dried, fresh, canned, baked – which one does your grandchild like the most?

7. VEGETABLE PEELERS: Give the children opportunities to learn how to use a vegetable peeler. Can they remove the skin of an apple all in one go? Can they make curls with carrots and celery? Yum!

8. FOLLOWING RECIPES: As your grandchild is able to read, they can pick out recipes they would like to make from your recipe books or cook books from the local library or online. For emergent readers, step by step cue cards with simple pictures may also do the trick!

9. COOKIES: Every child will have a favourite cookie so having them prepared when they come to visit is a great welcoming treat. Making them together is even better. Buying a cookie jar together to store all these treats is a great idea!

10. PANCAKES: Nothing is more fun than pouring out pancake mix into the shape of the first letter of your grandchild's name! Add faces to your pancake in the traditional round shape with fruit pieces.

11. PIZZAS: Pizzas can be made on English muffins and a wide range of healthy options. Begin with a tomato base then let your grandchild choose the toppings. Make happy faces or sad faces on the pizzas.

12. PASTA: Explore the variety of different types of pasta that are available and try some of them. Alphabet pasta is a great way to search for the letters in their name.

13. EDIBLE TIC TAC TOE: A variation on this popular game is to use bread sticks to create a much smaller board and use cucumbers for Os and crossed green beans for Xs and you get to eat the pieces as the game progresses.

14. INVENT A SANDWICH OR A SALAD: With harvest materials from the garden, the children may be interested in inventing a super sandwich or an incredible salad.

15. EDIBLE FLOWERS AND VEGETABLES: Create a salad, for example of vegetable florets and have edible flower petals for dessert. Paint pansy flowers with egg white then sprinkle on fine sugar and leave them to dry!

16. PICNICS: A picnic with all your favourites would be great fun in the summer but even more memorable if you have a winter picnic! Make it an eco friendly event and bring home all the containers leaving no garbage behind.

17. FROZEN TREATS: Making homemade ice milk, frozen yogurt, juice Popsicles and ice cream is always a favourite.

"Grandpas especially should have, stored in the refrigerator, some chocolate syrup. Grandmas (and mothers) usually complain (high sugar, etc.) but I don't care. The trick here is that it can't be chocolate milk, it has to be syrup so you can stand overtop of them at the table and pour it on to their ice cream (or in their milk) from 3 or 4 feet above their heads. Needless to say they love to stick their fingers in the stream and get an early taste!" MIKE, GRANDPARENT

18. SUN TEA: Use a large plastic jar with a lid and place the tea brewer on a dark surface that will absorb the sun. Fill the jar with water and add enough tea bags to make a good strong brew – experiment. If the sun is strong, the water will heat up and the tea will "cook". Add a few slices of lemon and allow the tea to steep for a few hours – then serve it up!

19. LET'S COOK: Use the bottom of a pizza box and line it with tin foil. Place the box in direct sunlight on a hot day (remind your grandchildren not to look directly into the sun) and try cooking a hot dog. An incredible example of solar power!

20. FOOD YOUR GRANDPARENTS MADE: Make foods for holidays and special occasions based on your memories of the past and your cultural heritage. Share these with your grandchildren.

21. RECIPE COLLECTION: Older grandchildren might like to create an online recipe collection of all of the family favourites for easy access.

22. FAMILY COOKBOOK: Create a document together with all of the family's favourite recipes as a gift for a special occasion. You might take photos of your grandchild preparing some of the recipes and the finished products to include in the cookbook.

23. BOOKS: There are so many wonderful children's books that lend themselves to food experiences. A great way to make a book come alive is to serve *Green Eggs and Ham* after reading the book by Dr. Seuss. Make porridge after reading *The Three Bears*, or making gingerbread men or a gingerbread house – a big project but delicious when finished after reading that story. Another classic is *Stone Soup* by Marcia Brown. Read the story then cook away!

 FURTHER READING:

Cloudy And The Chance Of Meatballs by Barrett
Mattie And The Peanut Butter Jelly Problem by Ames
Eating The Alphabet by Ehlert
Dragons' Alphabet Soup by Yu
Soup For Breakfast by Brown
50 Recipes For Kids To Cook: Food To Make Yourself Shown In Step-by-Step Pictures by Williams
PBS Kids Do It Myself Cookbook by PBS
50 Pizza Recipes by Rose
Noodle Kids: Around The World In 50 Fun, Healthy, Creative Recipes the Whole Family Can Cook Together by Sawyer
50 Super Easy Kids Recipes For Any Occasion by Andrews
201 Organic Baby And Toddler Meals: The Healthiest Toddler And Baby Food Recipes You Can Make by Gardiner

"Some of my happiest memories go back to Sunday dinners with my Italian grandmother, affectionately known as 'Nonna'. I would arrive at Nonna's house with the smell of simmering tomato sauce as she prepared spaghetti and meatballs. The majority of my time would be spent in the kitchen with Nonna, trying to figure out how she got the meatballs so tender and the sauce so savory and sweet. She was always happy to have me there and would let me taste the sauce and sneak me an extra meatball if I was lucky! Looking back at it now, it wasn't the food that I remember most; it was just being able to spend time with my Nonna." JON, GRANDSON

ARTS AND CRAFTS!

As with all experiences for young children it is very important to let them lead the play. Some activities such as knitting will require more help but when you can, model only as a last resort, encouraging creativity and their imagination. There is no right and wrong way of creating and nothing should take the place of inventive play where your grandchildren set their own agenda and choose their own open-ended materials. Using different materials allows for a richer experience. Many of these activities can be done in the outdoors helping to reduce the creative "mess"! You may also want to create a recycling box since many saved products are perfect for home projects. There is an important life lesson here about environmental awareness and our role in protecting our earth. You will also find that food has not been used in any of the activities presented in this section as in many cultures food is sacred.

ORGANIZERS: Create an interesting container for all your arts and craft supplies – a large Tupperware container, a six quart basket etc.

ESSENTIAL CRAFT SUPPLIES: Safety first – all items in your supplies and materials should be nontoxic. Some materials may be dangerous; for example, balloons can pop and be a choking hazard since the first thing many young children want to do is put objects in their mouth. Styrofoam meat trays should be avoided since they may be contaminated. Many of the items in your craft supply container will depend on the age of your grandchild and your budget but as you will see, many of these items are already in your home:

A PLACE TO PLAY: Small table and chairs, a TV tray, an art easel, sensory table or bin

PAINTING TOOLS: Old toothbrushes, paint rollers, feathers, combs, makeup brushes, house paint brushes, textured brushes, hair brushes, baby bottle brushes, paint trays, straws, toothpicks, squeeze bottles, spray bottles, screens, eye droppers, wooden tongue depressors, Popsicle sticks, sponges, tree branches

CONTAINERS: Use small stable containers with a brush in each colour, scoops

TRAYS: Use trays to contain the art work and for easy clean up

MESSY ACTIVITIES: Put some plastic or a plastic table cloth under the table or highchair

KITCHEN ITEMS: Paper plates, aluminum foil plates, sponges, pot scrubbers, cookie cutters, garlic press, rolling pin, measuring cups and spoons, rubber bands, sieve, funnels, paper bags, jelly molds, food colouring, tongs, egg cartons, corks, baster, liquid starch, cupcake liners

MESSY ACTIVITIES: Plastic apron or smock, big shirt, plastic gloves for really messy work, garbage bag with neck and arms cut out

PAINT: Tempera paint (add a drop of dish soap for easier clean up and less flaking when dry), washable finger paint, fluorescent finger paint, glitter paint, neon paint, metallic paint, washable water colours, washable sidewalk paint, oil paint, spray cans, varnish

THINGS TO PAINT ON: PAPER: Xerox, tissue, fingerpainting, crepe, coloured construction, corrugated, cardboard, chart, wrapping, rice, waxed, parchment, tissue, newspapers (from different cultural groups), boxes, magazines, comic strips, junk mail, wallpaper, paper plates, paper towels, cellophane, bristol board, and tin foil. Other Ideas: T-shirts, wood, clay, ceiling and floor tiles, juice or plastic lids, plexiglas, old placemats, window shades, venetian blinds, cloth, suede, vinyl, canvas, bubble wrap, doilies, old shower curtains, sidewalks

THINGS FOUND IN A SEWING BASKET: String, yarn, sequins, old spools of thread, fabric scraps, buttons, lace, Bodkin needles, feathers, pipe cleaners, felt, embroidery floss, chenille stems, pony beads, wood beads, glass beads, pom poms, googly eyes

GLUE: Glitter glue, water based white glue, super glue, wood glue, foam craft glue, glue dots and lines, glue sticks, sticker glue, rubber cement, hot glue gun for older children

TAPE: Masking tape, painter's tape, Scotch tape, duct tape, double sided tape

OFFICE ITEMS: Stapler, ruler, hole punch, blunt tip scissors for little ones, pinking shears, pointed tip scissors, fancy scissors for older children, stamps and stamp pads, stencils, foam sheets

THINGS TO MARK WITH:

Crayons - egg shaped, easy grip, triangular, jumbo, dry erase, fabric, twistable, mini, metallic FX, neon, glitter, window crayons, lead pencils, coloured pencils, watercolour pencils, charcoal sticks

MARKERS: Washable, smelly, broadline, fine tip, mini, glitter, fabric, gel, easy grip, dot, dry erase markers

PENS: Glitter, calligraphy, feathered, ball point, muti-functional, rollerball, patterned

CHALK: Anti-dust chalk, drawing, glitter, sidewalk, multi coloured sidewalk, washable chalk

THINGS FOUND IN THE BATHROOM: Tweezers, toilet paper rolls, cotton swabs, shaving cream, eye droppers

BEAUTIFUL JUNK

SAVE SOME OF THESE ITEMS FOR YOUR CRAFT EXPERIENCES:
acorns, artificial flowers, beads, boxes of all sizes, burlap, buttons, corks, coupons, confetti, candles, clothespins, coffee filters, cookie cutters, driftwood, dough press, dried flowers, eggshells, elastics, embroidery hoops, envelopes, funnels, food colouring, fabric dyes, garland, greeting cards, keys, locks, milk cartons, maps, magnifying glasses, netting, nylons, paper plates, pie plates, postcards, paint chips, paper bags, plastic pipes and tubes, rocks, ropes, ribbons, rickrack, rug samples, sandpaper, string, shoeboxes, stationery, shoelaces, screen wire, tiles, toothpicks, timers, tea strainers, tape measure, velvet, wool, wood scraps, wallpaper books, wire, yogurt containers, zippers.

FUN WITH PAINT

Simple Ideas

1. SENSORY BAGS: For very young children who may be reluctant to touch gooey activities, you can make a beginning by using a Ziploc bag and filling it with paint, playdough or any of the recipes listed in this book and allowing your grandchild to manipulate the bag. You can embed objects as well. Make sure that it is secured.

2. SHAKE IT UP: Save clear plastic water bottles for infants and toddlers in all shapes and sizes with different spouts, openings and fill them with interesting materials. In one of the bottles you might add water and oil and some food colouring, in others you might add water and corn syrup or hair gel, paint, tiny objects that are familiar to the child etc. Make sure they are securely closed by using a hot glue gun. This inexpensive idea will keep the children interested for a long time!

3. PAINT POTS: To help prevent a mess, put small amounts of paint into yogurt containers and place the pots inside a cardboard box with sides so that if they get tipped over it will help to contain the spills. You can also use a plastic egg carton to hold the paints.

4. MIX IT UP: Provide children with paints that when mixed together create a new colour, for example, yellow and blue make green, red and blue make purple etc.

5. BLOW PAINTING: Mix up some thin tempera paint and provide a straw and a big piece of paper. Spoon the tempera paint onto the paper and blow away. Adding several colours of paint makes for an interesting way of discovering how colours change when they are blended.

6. PAINTING WITH WATER: A great idea with little mess — provide a pail full of water and a big brush and let your children paint on the fence or sidewalk. On a hot day it is fun to watch the water evaporate.

7. FOLD OVER: Fold a piece of construction paper in half, open it up and place a dollop of paint on the middle crease. Fold closed and roll over it with a small paint roller. Open it up — wow!

8. SHAPE PAINTING: With a pie plate filled with paint, find a variety of objects of different shapes to put into the paint and then press the shapes onto white paper. Talk about the shapes. For extra fun try incorporating cookie cutters.

9. FINGERPAINTING: Fingerpaint on a cookie sheet with a piece of white paper cut to fit. The tray will help to contain the artist's masterpiece. Paint with shaving cream for a different texture then sprinkle on dry tempera paint for new colours.

10. EYE DROPPER PAINTING: A great way to encourage fine motor skills is providing a few colours of paint and several eye droppers. Your grandchild can create by squeezing the paint onto a paper.

11. SPONGE PAINTING: Find some thin sponges and cut them into different shapes. The shapes can then be dipped into containers of tempera paint and pushed onto paper to create interesting designs. When dry you might want to use it as wrapping paper.

12. MARBLE/GOLF PAINTING: Painting with marbles or golf balls on a tray lined with paper is great fun. Add a dollop of paint in the middle of the paper and add a variety of marbles in different shapes and/or golf balls. Roll and tip the tray and watch what happens!

13. STRING PAINTING: Collect a variety of different pieces of string, wool or shoe laces and dip them into a variety of colours of paint. Drag the string across the paper – you could even pretend you are dragging snakes!

14. PRINTS: Gently place a piece of white paper on top of one of their masterpieces, lift off and you have a new picture to frame.

15. HAND PRINTS: When fingerpainting, don't let those gooey handprints go to waste, create greeting cards or wrapping paper by placing their hands on some interesting paper.

16. FOOT PRINTS: Creating foot prints is a great warm day experience. Have the children in bare feet, encourage them to step in the paint and go on a walk about on a long piece of butcher paper. Supervise carefully as it can get slippery. A hose at the end makes for easy clean up.

17. MAKING TRACKS: Line a tray with a piece of white paper. Pour on some paint and let your grandchildren use their wheeled vehicles to run through the paint.

18. BUBBLE ART: You can also put bubble solution and a small amount of food colouring into a large plastic container and give your grandchild a straw. Blow into the solution then capture the masterpiece by laying a piece of white paper over the bubbles.

19. ROCK PAINTING: Collect all those favourite rocks and paint them!

"Grandparenting has all the benefits of parenthood without the daily responsibility - in other words, it's great!"
TERRY, GRAMPA

More complex Ideas

1. SPLATTER PAINTING: This is definitely an outside idea. You may show your grandchildren pictures of famous artists and their work, for example Jackson Pollock. You can use a variety of paint brushes and tempera paint to splatter away. You may want to hang their artwork on a fence for drying and to show off their artistic talents!

2. LEAF PRINTING: Paint leaves on one side and press them onto a plain table cloth, napkins, butcher block paper or card stock for some amazing designs. Use a wide range of leaves and different colours for the best effect!

3. WRAPPING PAPER: Place leaves on a large piece of paper and dab paint from a sponge over the top of the leaves. When the leaves are lifted off, the silhouette will be there. The same idea can be done with paint, a small piece of wire mesh and an old toothbrush. The brush is dipped into the paint, rubbed over the wire mesh to create a spatter painting. When the leaves are removed a wonderful impression is made.

4. LEAF TREASURES: Find a variety of beautiful fall leaves and place them between two sheets of clear contact paper. Punch holes and hang them in the window.

5. BOOK COVER: Create marbleized paper by pouring a little oil paint on a water surface in a dishpan. Stir with a wooden stir stick and when the pattern is just right,

lay a sheet of paper on the surface and carefully lift it off. Set to dry. When dry, use the paper to cover a special book or use as wrapping paper. Oil based paint is permanent so be careful!

6.   NEW FACES: Buy face make-up to paint faces. This would be a great time to look up characters in Chinese opera, the Kabuki style theater of Japan or the Nuba of Sudan for ideas and lots of discussions.

7.   HANDPRINTS: Using the salt clay recipe, use a rolling pin to roll out the dough. Have your grandchild press their hand firmly into the clay. If you want you can carve the date and the child's name into the clay. Let it dry and paint. You can also put favourite shells, rocks or other treasures into the clay.

8.   CRAYOLA'S AIR DRY CLAY: For a quick and easy product to work with, try using this clay. It is smoother and less sticky than traditional clay and you don't need to use the oven. It is also easy to clean up from little hands and surfaces.

9.   TREASURE BOX: Dollars stores carry small to large wooden boxes. These can be decorated and become a box that holds treasures from beach walks, favourite marbles, stones or any other treasure.

10. FANCY JARS: Glass paints are available and as a special gift your grandchildren might like to make jam or preserves and decorate the bottles to be given for a special occasion for a loved one.

11. COFFEE FILTERS: Fold coffee filters into interesting shapes and dip a corner into some food colouring. Watch the colour "bleed" through the filter. Try using different folds and other colours of food colouring. You might want to do this with plastic gloves!

 FUN WITH PAPER

Simple Ideas

1.   CRAYONS AND PAPER: For many children, their first experiences with art materials are crayons and paper. Crayons now come in large sizes for little hands.

"The most important thing is to sit with your grandchildren. I like to ask if I can colour too. I think they like being the boss because I usually get a 'yes' but it comes with lots of instructions - I'm not allowed to pick my own colour, they do that for you too!" MIKE, GRANDFATHER

2. SCISSOR FUN: For little hands just learning to use their scissors, prepare thin strips of stiff paper so that with one snip they will be successful!

3. COLLAGE: You can create an interesting piece of art by letting the children help themselves to materials that interest them. They can tear or cut and all you need to

do is provide lots of glue. They might also use items they have collected on a nature walk or items in your sewing basket.

4. PAPER STRIPS: Try cutting a variety of construction paper strips of paper and show your grandchild how to pleat them or curl them with a pencil and then glue away for a 3D effect or use them to make rings.

5. CROWNS: Cut a band of construction paper and measure your grandchild's head for a good fit. Decorate away using markers, sequins, feathers, plastic jewels etc. and tape closed.

6. MARVELOUS PLACE MATS: Create placemats for the table by using contact paper, placing photos or drawings on the bottom sheet then placing another piece of paper on top, press and seal! Presto! Drawings made by your grandchildren can also be laminated at a local printing shop. A great way to preserve their art work integrated into everyday use.

More complex Ideas

1. MY BODY: Roll out a long sheet of butcher block paper and have your grandchild lie down. Trace around the child's body and have him or her cut it out or help if needed. Your grandchildren can then draw themselves on the paper with clothes, label the body parts etc.

2. FAVOURITE FOODS: Have your grandchild cut out pictures from magazines of their favourite foods and glue them onto a paper plate. Make some for supper!

3. NIFTY NAPKIN RINGS: You can make napkin rings by cutting up toilet paper rolls and having your grandchild decorate with markers, fabric and lots of glue!

4. CARDS: Children can make greeting cards for many occasions by decorating a folded piece of construction paper. Use a variety of interesting materials to make outstanding cards.

5. TISSUE PAPER ART: Tissue paper is very inexpensive and easy to tear so you can provide a variety of colours and glue the pieces on paper or on a Mason jar and presto a fabulous piece of art! For durability cover the jar with Mod Podge.

6. MARDI GRAS: Celebrate by making a full face mask using a strong paper plate, cutting out spaces for eyes and a large triangle for the mouth. Decorate with glue and lots and lots of feathers, sequins, and sparkles. Punch holes on either side and stick on white reinforcements then attach ribbons. Smaller masks can also be created by measuring and cutting out a mask to fit just over the eyes. Lots of shapes are possible such as a cat shape.

7. PAPER MACHE MASKS: These can be made by mixing together 1 part flour, 1 part salt and 1 part water into a thick and goopy paste. Blow up a balloon and place strips of newspaper dipped in the Paper Mache (squeeze off excess glue) on one half of the balloon. Leave holes for eyes, nose and mouth. Paint and decorate when dry.

8. BOOK MARKS: Decorate and make book marks with a favourite quotation on each. They might also be created in the shape of their favourite dinosaur, truck, animal, fish etc. Punch a hole in the end and add a ribbon.

9. SKETCHING: Give your grandchildren clip boards (nothing makes them feel more important) and graphite pencils, charcoal etc and encourage them to sketch their favourite plant or flower. Take a photo of the flower and post with their drawings or just provide the materials for them to decide on their own what they would like to sketch.

10. ORIGAMI: Older children may enjoy creating Origami boxes, flowers, animals etc. All they need is Origami paper and a good Origami book to help them along.

 FURTHER READING:

Origami For Children: 35 Easy To Follow Step-By-Step Projects by Ono
The ABCs Of Origami: Paper Folding For Children by Sarasas
Easy Origami by Montroll
Origami For Beginners: The Creative World Of Paper Folding by Temko
Origami Greeting Cards by Asahi

11. SCRAPBOOKING: You might like to create a scrapbook together to hold your favourite works of art, stories, and photos. Lots of scrapbook props can be bought to add colour and creativity to your project. Martha Stewart has some great ideas for scrapbooking. Check out marthastewart.com for more fun projects!

@ www.marthastewart.com/274963/scrapbook-ideas-and-albums/@ center/276976/memorykeeping-crafts

 ## FUN WITH NATURE

Simple Ideas

1. PUMPKIN PAINTING: Nothing like painting the pumpkin you have grown!

2. BUTTERFLIES: Create a clothes pin butterfly using brightly coloured tissue paper, gather it in the middle and clip it together with a clothes pin. You can add pipe cleaners for antennae and googly eyes etc. onto the clothes pin. Stickers can be applied to the wings for an even more spectacular butterfly.

3. STONE SCULPTURES/INUKSHUKS: Choose rocks of different sizes, shapes and colours. Have the children pick the rocks that are the most interesting to them. Encourage the children to make rock sculptures providing them with lots of rubber cement. A great opportunity to discuss balance, gravity, tipping point etc. Some children may want to paint, add props or other creative materials to their Inukshuk. They might want to create an Inukshuk garden with all their structures strategically placed. Take their photos and display their creativity.

4. OCEAN PICTURES: On a piece of paper your grandchild might like to create a beach scene with sand and pebbles or their favourite fish with their crayons. When they are finished, have them paint over their pictures with watered down blue tempera paint. Hang to dry!

5. LEAF TIARAS: Buy some plastic head bands from the dollar store. When the leaves are falling bring a variety of leaves to your work table and have the children create their own magical tiaras with lots of glue! You might want to include other fall items such as acorns, maple keys etc.

6. SUN REFLECTORS: Use a square of aluminum foil glued on a sturdy square of cardboard to create reflections on a sunny day. A variation could be using small unbreakable mirrors.

"Whenever I would come into a room, my grandmother's face would light up. She loved me unconditionally despite all evidence to the contrary!" JAMIL, GRANDSON

More complex Ideas

1. EGG CARTONS: Rinsed plastic egg cartons can be cut up into individual pieces or used whole to create all kinds of creepy critters — use pipe cleaners, sequins, buttons, beads and lots and lots of white glue!

2. RUBBINGS: Rubbings are a fun activity during the fall when there are many leaves on the ground! Encourage your grandchild to find their favourite leaves. Bring them back home and place the leaves on the table and place a piece of white paper on top (taping the leaf down may help to keep it in place). Take the side of a crayon, charcoal, or a pencil or chalk and rub away. You may need to help by holding down the paper. This may expand into a bigger experience as children find other objects both inside and outside the house to rub. A big favourite is old coins. You can also use corrugated cardboard for an interesting rubbing experience.

3. WREATH MAKING: Collect a variety of interesting fall items, acorns, leaves, twigs and glue them on a Styrofoam ring and create a wreath for the entrance to your home. Another idea is to use bendable vines such as wisteria, Virginia creeper etc and bend it around a large ball or round container and once you have wrapped it around several times, slip it off the ball and use twist ties to keep the vine together. Now comes the fun part, decorate with seasonal items.

4. WINDOW ART: A simple idea is to use plastic lids from containers and decorate the lids by drawing on it with markers or cutting up cellophane paper into interesting shapes and gluing them on the lid. When done, punch a hole in the top, add string and hang it in the window. A good time to sing "You Are My Sunshine" or "Mr Sun, Sun Mister Golden Sun".

5. VOLCANOES: Nothing is more fun than mixing vinegar and baking soda together to create explosions. An activity best done outside in the sand box!

6. POTPOURRI GIFTS: Collect leaves and flower petals – rose buds and petals, lavender flowers, geranium, lemon balm, peony, phlox, daylilies, lilac etc. Set them out to dry but not in direct sunlight. When dry, grind them up or put them in a blender. Place the collection in woven mesh bags, tie and decorate with ribbons.

7. MOBILES: After a walk to the beach you may want to create a fish mobile. A simple hanger can be used covered with ribbon. Cut out a variety of fish shapes and have your grandchild decorate each fish. Provide a wide range of materials to allow their imagination to soar. When completed, punch a hole in the middle of each fish and using thin ribbon or fishing line for a more transparent look, hang each of the fish from the hanger. A great idea for an older grandchild to create one of these for a new baby in the family to be hung over their crib.

"My fondest memories of my own grandparents were made from being able to share their passions. When they share their passion with you it becomes magical. My Grandfather made Christmas decorations out of tree bark and pine cones and they seemed like the art of Picasso." KARYN, GRANDDAUGHTER

ELABORATE CRAFTS

TRADITIONAL CRAFTS: For many children they are no longer exposed to crafts that we grew up with. Perhaps you can continue the tradition by teaching children to knit, macramé, cork, cross stitch, embroider, building projects etc.

Simple Ideas

1. BEADING: Even young children can enjoy stringing very large beads with a pipe cleaner and then with a shoelace but older children may enjoy making bracelets and necklaces from a wide variety of different beads. Watch young children carefully for choking issues.

2. BEAD NECKLACES: Using the salt clay recipe, encourage your grandchild to roll a small piece of clay in their hands until it is perfectly round and the right size for their necklace. Push a nail through the centre of the ball then let the balls dry. Then the beads can be painted and using a bodkin needle and yarn, thread through all the balls to make the necklace. You can use pieces of straws in between the beads for a different effect.

3. STRAW NECKLACES: You can buy a box of colourful straws and cut them into lengths. Children can use Gymp since it comes in many colours or a long shoelace or thin elastic to make an interesting necklace.

4. NAME BRACELETS: Use Gymp and thread on plastic block letter beads to spell out name bracelets for their family and friends and even their grandparents!

5. WEAVING: Collect plastic berry baskets and weave ribbon or yarn in and out through the holes. This creates a pretty holder for special items.

6. TOOTH FAIRY: You never know when a child might lose a tooth so be prepared by creating a tooth fairy pillow to tuck in the tooth and in the morning – presto – a Loonie in its place!

7. STRING GAMES: String games increase children's creativity and dexterity. All you need is string! There are many interesting books about string games.

 FURTHER READING:

> *Cat's Cradle, Owl's Eyes: A Book Of String Games by Gryski*
> *Many Stars And More String Games by Gryski*
> *Pull The Other One: String Games And Stories by Taylor*
> *String Games by Darsie*

8. BOXES BIG AND SMALL: We have all seen young children play endlessly with boxes rather than the gift inside. Save large appliance boxes and create your own puppet theatre, car, castle or space ship.

9. FIND THE TREASURE BOX: Design together a wonderful treasure box from an old shoe box or Dollar Store wooden box. Then you might play the game "Hot or Cold" by hiding the treasure box before your grandchild comes to visit. They

can search for the box while you say hot if they are getting close and cold if they are moving away from the box. This goes on until you say for example, "you are burning up" and then they locate the box. Make sure there is a surprise inside.

10. STAMPS: Used stamps can be bought in bulk. The children can sort them in all kinds of ways.

11. MAKE MUSICAL INSTRUMENTS: Old coffee cans, pots and pans and wooden spoons can be the basis for your own marching band. What other items in the kitchen make interesting noises?

12. HEADBANDS AND BARRETTES: You can purchase simple plain headbands and barrettes and with a collection of artificial flowers, glue away.

13. BULLETIN BOARD: Create a bulletin board together that is just for your grand-child. Post all important messages of upcoming events at home, school and in their community. A great spot for artwork as well.

"Grandchildren are your reward for having children!"
JUDI, GRAND-MERE

14. SIDEWALK CHALK: Decorating the sidewalk with multi-coloured chalk with pictures or hop scotch is great fun!

 FURTHER READING:

Chalk by Thomson
Chalk Box Kid by Bulla
A Piece Of Chalk by Ericsson
The Chalk Drawings Mystery by Murphy
Sidewalk Chalk. Outdoor Fun And Games by McGillian

More complex Ideas

1. KNITTING: Knitting a scarf to keep warm may take some time for beginners but you may be able to provide the necessary instructions. Crochet, corking, macrame are also options. Visiting a wool store is an experience in itself!

2. A MEMORY QUILT: A memory quilt can be a reflection of a child's life by integrating clothing your grandchild no longer wears but were favourites. You might also ask the child to decorate a square with fabric crayons every year on their birthday. You could save them and create a new quilt at an important time in the child's life – off to college or university, their 18th birthday or as a wedding gift.

3. DECORATE T-SHIRTS: All you need are plain white T-shirts and fabric markers and you are good to go! You may want to create a shirt by creating a family crest with older grandchildren or a birthday T-shirt for a parent or friend.

4. DYING: Take a white t-shirt or a pair of white socks and twist them up and secure the twist with elastic. Mix up some cold water dye in your grandchild's favourite colour and dip the items into the dye. Stir them about, then squeeze out the excess liquid, and hang to dry. Presto – new clothes to wear!

5. BAD DREAMS: Many children at some point or another are worried about monsters and demons in their rooms. A Dream Catcher in the window may help to alleviate these fears. The story of the Dream Catcher is an important link to our Aboriginal teachers and should be treated with great respect. More information is available at

@ www.dream-catchers.org/dream-catchers-faq.php

6. MARKING TERRITORY: If you have the space, this is a great way for your grandchildren to put their mark on their grandparent's place. A totem lets everyone know who "lives" there. A totem can be made by cutting sonotubes into rounds and the children then decorate each section of the totem, put them all together with tape and anchor them outside in an appropriate spot.

7. CREATIVE CANDLES: An activity that takes lots of supervision but with great results. The David Suzuki Foundation shows you how to make candles in a safe and non-toxic manner.

@ www.davidsuzuki.org/publications/downloads/2011/Queen-of-Green-candlemaking.pdf

"I loved my grandparent's home and it was the best place to be when I felt sad. I was safe there." AMIR, GRANDSON

8. FANCY FEET: Inexpensive flip flops can be made into amazing foot-wear by adding ribbons, bows, large sequins, tulle etc. with a hot glue gun. Supervise carefully!

9. ART FROM RECYCLABLES: Give each of your grandchildren a bag filled with recyclables such as plastic utensils, paper or Styrofoam cups, paper rolls, rubber bands, twist ties, drinking straws, lengths of string or yarn, Styrofoam trays (not meat), packing "peanuts" etc (This activity should only be done with older children as Styrofoam cannot be detected in an X-ray if it is swallowed). Children should have access to paper, scissors, tape, glue etc. The children are encouraged to create something creative or useful with all of their items.

 FURTHER READING:

Recycled Crafts Box by Martin
Gorgeous Gifts: Use Recycled Material To Make Cool Crafts by Craig
Creative Costumes by Craig
Ecocrafts: Jazzy Jewelry by Craig
Bottle Cap Activities by Cisnieros

10. MY SPACE: Some grandchildren may really enjoy the idea of creating a door sign that signals that this is their room either at home or when they visit you. They might like to choose a theme, one of their favourite interests at the time – dinosaurs, space ships, flowers etc to decorate their sign with their name boldly displayed. More signs can be made if the children are sharing a room. The sign could be a shape that goes right on the door or a shape with a hook on the end that goes around the door knob.

11. MAKE A BOARD GAME: When your grandchildren are bored with your board games, try making one up.

12. DECORATE TABLEWARE: You can create interesting plates, cups and saucers, mugs etc on plain white china with permanent china markers. These plates can be used for every visit to Granny and Grampa's house!

13. WINTER CLOTHING: Older children might enjoy a head band made out of felt with Velcro at the ends. It can be decorated with gems and jewels!

"My grandmother was a seamstress in the old country and one of my best memories is of the time we spent together making my dress for the prom. She made me look and feel beautiful at a time when I didn't feel that way about myself. I will never forget the tears in her eyes as I walked out the door! She was the best!" MAEVE, PARENT

FUN RECIPES

1. PLAYDOUGH: 1 cup cold water, 1 cup salt, 2 teaspoons vegetable oil, 2 cups flour, 2 tablespoons cornstarch. Mix water, salt and oil then mix in flour and cornstarch adding a little bit at a time. Adjust as you go and knead together at the end. Add interesting props – a pasty wheel, apple slicer, garlic press, plastic knives, cookie cutters etc. Keep the playdough wrapped to preserve it and keep it in an airtight container. For added interest you can add other elements to the playdough – food colouring (add it to the water), sparkles, peppermint oil, almond or vanilla extract etc.

2. GOOP – Cornstarch and water make a deliciously "goopy" substance that feels wet and dry all at the same time. Experiment with amounts.

3. SALT DOUGH: 1 cup salt, 1 ½ cups water, 4 cups flour, 4 tablespoons cooking oil. You can roll this out and use interesting cookie cutters to create shapes. Bake for 45

minutes at 350 degrees. Poke a hole in it before you put it in the oven so you can hang it in the window, on the Christmas tree etc. Varnish or paint with acrylic paint.

4. CORNSTARCH GLUE: 3 tablespoons cornstarch, 4 tablespoons cold water, and 2 cups hot water. Mix the cornstarch and cold water in a pot and when smooth slowly pour in the hot water and keep stirring. Heat until it thickens, keep stirring. Remove from heat and let cool. You can pour it into a squeeze bottle and store in the refrigerator.

5. BOUNCY BALL: Borax, cornstarch and glue makes a bouncy ball - who knew! Use an 8 oz glue bottle and empty it into a bowl. Fill the empty bottle with warm water and shake. Pour it into the bowl and mix with the glue. Add food colouring at this stage. In a separate bowl, add ½ cup water and stir in 1 teaspoon of borax. Slowly add this mixture to the glue. Store in a Ziplock bag for future use.

6. BREAD CRITTERS: Use 1 cup of water, 1 cup of salt, and 3 cups of flour. Knead all the ingredients together and break off parts of the dough to create your bread critters, add items to make them unique. Bake at 275 degrees for 2-3 hours, watch them carefully while in the oven. When they are cool they can be painted.

7. SILLY PUTTY: This is a messy but really fun activity with dramatic results. Mix together 2 parts of white glue and 1 part liquid starch and some food colouring. Alter the ingredients until it is just right, for example if it is too stiff, add more starch. Chill for a few hours then play away!

8. FINGERPAINT: Use 1 cup of liquid laundry starch along with ½ cup of powdered tempera paint. Add a few drops of food colouring for a different effect.

9. THREE D PAINT: Mix 1 cup of soap flakes and ½ cup cold water and a few drops of food colouring. Put the first two ingredients into a bowl and use an electric mixer to mix until the mixture is stiff. Add the food colouring at the end. The consistency when dry gives a three dimensional look.

10. LEMONADE: Lemons, water and sugar to taste.

 FURTHER READING:

The Lemonade War by Davies
The Lemonade Crime by Davies

The Lemonade Club by Polacco
Lulu's Lemonade by deRubertis
Lemonade And Other Poems Squeezed From A Single Word by Raczka

11. SAND SCULPTURE: You need a spoon, saucepan, 500 ml of sand, 250 ml of cornstarch, and 250 ml of water. Mix the sand, cornstarch, and water together in a pan. Heat over low heat and keep stirring. Remove when the mixture is thick. Let it cool and begin the sculpting. Let it dry to harden.

"My Grandmother always tried to make playdough when we came over to her house. Somehow the recipe was never right, it was either stiff as a board or so sticky we couldn't get it off our fingers. It became a family joke and still makes me smile years later." BERNADETTE, PARENT

"Buried somewhere in a closet is my handprint on a plate. My grandmother's greatest treasure!" ARIANNA, PARENT

DRESS UP AND DRAMATIC PLAY

There is so much to learn from observing children engaged in dramatic play. You may gain insight into the challenges your grandchild might be facing since many children act out their feelings during play situations. It is an important outlet for children from toddlers to schoolage. Add props as their play develops. Become a play partner by letting your grandchild lead the play but don't forget to dress up as well! Older grandchildren will love to do your makeup and hair! Be a good sport!

"When my parents divorced, the only place I really felt safe was at my grandparent's house. There was no arguing, no fighting just a safe calm place for me to just be."
ADANNA, GRANDDAUGHTER

Simple Ideas

1. MAGICAL CLOSET: A fun idea is to gather up glow in the dark sticks, flashlights etc. and hide in the closet. This could be a place to read books by flashlight or a camping light fastened on a headband. You might even add some glow in the dark stick-ons like stars and moons to the walls and the ceiling!

2. UNDER THE TABLE: If you are a sewer you might design a covering that fits right over a small table that includes a window and a door for entry. Take in the tea set or a box of wheeled vehicles and you are good to go.

3. FANCY CLOTHES: Add new items (check out garage sales or ask for donations from your friends) to your stash of fun things to dress up in – feather boas, saris, belts, jewels, scarves, gloves, capes, hats, wigs, handbags, brief cases, bow ties, high heel shoes, crowns etc.

 FURTHER READING:

Curious George Goes To A Costume Party by Rey
Mardi Gras: Parades, Costumes And Parties by Landau

4. HATS: It is easy to create props for dramatic play, for example a princess hat can be made by creating a cone shape from heavy paper. Before taping it closed decorate the circle shape with markers or by gluing on pieces of tissue paper then measure it on your grandchild's head then tape or staple it closed. Add some ribbons or crepe paper strips and it's good to go! Another option might be to take a paper plate and glue on fancy items from your arts and crafts box. Punch a hole on either side of the plate (reinforce with white reinforcements) and add ribbon. You can make crowns for kings or queens by measuring and cutting a crown to fit and decorate away! Hats of all kinds are great fun, favourite baseball hats are always a hit!

5. SUN GLASSES: Collect old sunglasses in all shapes, sizes and colours. Compare, sort and discuss how sunglasses make the world look different. Take photos of your grandchild!

6. RESTAURANT: Dramatic play with a restaurant theme is always a great hit. You might set up a small corner in your home or apartment to encourage this experience. You will need plastic cups and plates, plastic cutlery, napkins, pots and pans, serving utensils, place mats, old food boxes and cans (be careful of sharp edges), note pad and pencil for taking your order etc. Using real food, your grandchild may be able to serve you something interesting in his or her restaurant.

7. STAGE PUPPET SHOWS/PLAYS/MUSICALS/FASHION SHOW/ KARAOKE: An outdoor veranda may be the perfect place to stage any of these

events. There is nothing more compelling than an interested audience. If the audience is limited you can always line up some stuffed animals!

8. PUPPETS READY TO GO: A shoe storage bag is a great way to organize and make puppets accessible to the children.

9. PAPER BAG PUPPETS: Brown paper lunch bags make are perfect for little hands. Decorate and you are good to go!

10. SPOON PUPPETS: The Dollar Store often has wooden spoons in packages of three in different sizes so you can create a variety of puppet friends. Use markers to

draw on faces, use yarn for hair and place a fabric around the spoon for clothing. You can also paint the handle.

11. FAIRY PUPPETS: Make a fairy puppet by folding a piece of strong paper in half and draw a wing shape on it and cut along the lines. Open it up and you have wings! Cut out a head, arms, legs and clothes. Decorate then glue all the body parts on a straw. You can also enhance the wings once they have been cut out by placing a blob of paint in the centre of the fold and press or use a paint roller. Open up and you have very amazing wings.

12. FINGER PUPPETS: Draw a face on your grandchild's index finger. Play away.

13. FINGER PUPPETS FROM GLOVES: A simple idea for a pair of used rubber gloves – cut the fingers off the glove and draw on interesting faces. You now have 10 characters for your puppet show.

14. STICK PUPPETS: Decorate a paper towel roll with paint or markers and add on googly eyes, hair from yarn or by curling paper strips etc. You can use tongue depressors or Popsicle sticks glued inside the roll for a handle.

15. SOCK PUPPETS: Find a long knee high sock and have your grandchild fill the sock with crumpled newspaper. Tie off and at the other end tie a section for the head with yarn or string. Add some googly eyes and a piece of red felt for the tongue securing tightly.

16. BABY PUPPETS: Young children are often keen on learning more about babies of all kinds, human as well as animals. A visit to a local farm or zoo will facilitate this. Puppets of common animals are also available in most toy stores to enhance this experience.

 FURTHER READING:

Head, Shoulders, Knees And Toes, Baby Board Book by Kubler
Baby's Book Of The Body by Priddy
Go Baby by Steckel
Baby Farm Animals by Williams
Baby Animals. Baby Touch and Feel by Sirett
Chuckling Ducklings And Baby Animal Friends by Zenz
Animal Babies Around The House by Weber

More complex Ideas

1. PROP BOXES: Prop boxes can be organized and stored but ready when an interest is sparked. For example you could have a *jewelry box* that includes necklaces, clip on earrings, rings, bracelets, and unbreakable mirrors. Another idea would be a *housekeeping* prop box with dolls, a doll's bed, clothes for the dolls, blankets, pots and pans, dishes and utensils, baby bottles, empty food containers, measuring spoons and cups, wooden spoons, spatulas, cake pans, muffin tins, mixing bowls, aprons, dish cloths, sponges etc. For your musical grandchild, a *sound box* can be filled with instruments and homemade props such as a wooden ring with bells attached with ribbons, shaker bottles, small pots and lids and a soup spoon. Can't find a good box, not to worry a pillow case will do the same. Here are some other ideas for prop boxes and some books to go along with them:

2. BAKING BOX – playdough, empty food containers, aprons, oven mitts, chef hats, muffin tins, muffin paper cups, empty baking items – cake mixes, Brownies, muffins etc., cake pans, cookie sheet, spatulas, spoons, measuring spoons, measuring cups, rolling pins, mixing bowls, dish cloths, tea towels, funnels, egg cartons, baking soda and baking powder empty containers, empty vanilla container, egg beater, flour sifter, cookie cutters, icing bags, birthday candles, bottle opener, cook books, timer, cash register.

 FURTHER READING:

Five Little Monkeys Bake A Birthday Cake by Christelow
Walter The Baker by Carle
Super Duper Cupcakes by Cohen

3. PIZZA BOX – discarded pizza boxes, Easy Bake stove/oven, round cardboard pizza circles for the children to decorate, toppings made from felt, pizza cutter, order pad, cash register, "money", telephone, apron, chef's hat, table, cutlery, red and white table cloth, menu – wouldn't it be so much more meaningful if the children could be making real pizzas!

FURTHER READING:

Let's Make Pizza In The Kitchen by Children's Press
The Pizza Mystery (The Boxcar Children
Mysteries #33) by Chandler Warner
Babies Don't Eat Pizza by Danzig & Tilley
Pizza Counting by Dobson
Pizza At Sallys by Wellington

4. SCHOOL BOX: Playing school is often popular so a box with a chalkboard, erasers and chalk, stickers, notebooks, interesting pens and pencils and markers, binders, stamps and ink pads, interesting paper, calculator, file folders, envelopes, hole punch.

 FURTHER READING:

Going To School by Civardi
The Night Before Preschool by Wing
Curious George's First Day of School by Rey
David Goes To School by Shannon

5. BALL BOX – ping pong balls, rubber sponge balls, tennis balls, beach balls, soccer balls, footballs, rugby balls, soft balls, Koosh balls, cricket ball, golf balls, whiffle balls, anti-stress balls, foam balls, inflated balls, balls that light up when squeezed, red/white and blue balls, textured balls, balls with numbers such as pool balls, balls with shapes etc.

 FURTHER READING:

Stop That Ball by McClintock and Siebel
Where Is Baby's Beach Ball? by Katz
Magic School Bus Plays Ball by Cole
Elmo's World: Balls! by Barrett
Play Ball Amelia Bedelia by Parish

6. PLAY DOUGH BOX – Consider including play dough wrapped tightly, pastry wheels, plastic place mats, cookie cutters, popsicle sticks, tongue depressors, rolling pins, plastic knives, plastic scissors, scissors with different cutting blades, garlic press, plastic pizza cutter, wire mesh, sieve, muffin tins, small animals, vehicles etc.

FURTHER READING:

Make Your Own Playdough, Paint And Other Craft Materials by Caskey
The Rainy Day Activity Book by Rader
The Party by Reid
Fox Walked Alone by Reid
The Subway Mouse by Reid

7. PICNIC BOX – Don't just think summer, consider a winter picnic as well and include a blanket, chair, picnic basket, colourful plastic cups and dishes, napkins, lemonade, sunscreen, thermos, coolers, beach umbrella, inner tubes, air mattress, beach towels, sunglasses, straw hats, beach ball, delicious treats and teddy bears for a Teddy Bear Picnic!

FURTHER READING:

Teddy Bears' Picnic by Kennedy
Halmoni And The Picnic by Nyul Choi
We're Going On A Picnic by Hutchins
Ants On A Picnic by Dahl
A Picnic In October by Bunting

8. CAMPING BOX – tents or sheets, big clips for fastening, blankets, logs, red-orange cellophane for fire, sleeping bag, pillow cases, backpack, cooler, cereal boxes, granola bar boxes, trail mix, frying pan, pots, thermos, plates, cups, cutlery, spatula, tongs, marshmallows, lanterns, glow sticks, fishing rod, blue tarp to be a lake, folding chairs, camera, swim suits, flashlight, maps, binoculars, sunglasses, mosquito net, stuffed animals.

FURTHER READING:

Curious George Goes Camping by Rey
Amelia Bedelia Goes Camping by Parish & Sweat
Camping Out by Mayer
When We Go Camping by Ruurs & Kiss
A Camping Spree With Mr. Magee by Van Dusen

9. TREASURE BOX — a map, rocks, nuggets (paint small rocks gold), coloured stones and gems, coins, marbles, old jewelry, casket, keys, pirate hat, eye patch, black boots, bandanas, scarves, belts, goblet, feathered parrot. You might also create a secret pirate map using lemon juice and a Q-tip, dip it into the lemon juice and write out your message. The message will appear when you heat the paper with an iron. Go to this web site for a pattern for creating a pirate hat:

www.leehansen.com/printables/masks/pirate-hat-craft-sheet.pdf

FURTHER READING:

Pirates Don't Change Diapers by Long and Shannon
How I Became A Pirate by Long & Shannon
Do Pirates Take Baths? By Tucker
Shiver Me Letters: A Pirate's ABC by Sobel
Pirate Pete by Kennedy

10. TRAVEL BOX — This box would be great fun just before a real travel adventure with your grandchild - suitcases, travel brochures, maps, posters, old airline tickets, outdated passports, old phone cards, beach hats, towels, beach balls, plastic sun-glasses, terry robes, sandals, paper, pencils, camera, sun hats, sunscreen, small travel kit - shampoo bottles, toothbrushes, toothpaste, brush, comb, sunscreen, "money", postcards, travel magazines, fins, snorkels, beach umbrella.

FURTHER READING:

All You Need For A Beach by Schertle
Kids Trip Diary by Bree
Stories and Legends Of Travel And History For Children by Greenwood
When Daddy Travels by Ziefert & Bolam
When Mommy Travels by Ziefert & Bolam

11. MAGIC TRICKS: At some point most children are interested in magic tricks. There are a number of simple books and videos on how to carry off these tricks.

"I love being a grandma! You can be silly, play Hide and Seek forever and let your grandchildren jump on your bed!!! Most parents are too busy for the silly side of life but grandparents usually have all the time in the world and generally more patience." JUDI, GRAND-MERE

MUSIC AND MOVEMENT

FURTHER READING:

Games Children Sing Around The World by Ramsier

Old Fashion Children's Games by O'Brien

Singing Games Children Love by Gagne

Hush Baby Hush, Lullabies From Around The World by Henderson

The Laughing Baby: Songs And Rhymes From Around The World
    by Scott

Music Music For Everyone by Williams

101 Rhythm Instrument Activities For Young

Children by Flesch Connors & Wright

Kids Make Music: Clapping And Tapping From Bach

To Rock by Hart, Mantell, Trezzo Braren

Music For Ones And Twos: Songs and Games

For The Very Young Child by Glazer

Dancing In My Bones by Andrews

101 Dance Games For Children by Rooyackers & Hurd

Simple Ideas

1. SING ALL THE TIME: Sing together, it heals.

2. MUSIC OUTSIDE: Take your music outside – a tape recorder, your smart phone, your portable sound system and sing and dance away.

3. MOVING TO THE GROOVE: Listen to some music, ask your grandchildren how it make them feel, then ask them to move to it. You could put together some really contrasting music moving from rock, to hip hop, to rap, to jazz, to classic for some really interesting interpretations.

4. MARCHING BAND: Create some homemade instruments and create your own parade. You might even want to create some marching band clothes to go along with it – fancy hats, a baton etc and sing along – *The Ants Go Marching, The Grand Old Duke of York* etc.

5. INSTRUMENTS: Make instruments from old large coffee tins that can become a drum, water bottles with small rocks inside, a tambourine made from an embroidery hoop with bells fastened on, pots and pans, lids, wooden spoons etc. Look for anything that makes a noise.

6. FREEZE TO MUSIC: Play a familiar song and stop the music. Encourage the child to freeze and hold that position.

7. LET'S DANCE: Teach your grandchildren some steps from your favourite dance moves – "The Mash Potatoes", "The Twist". Do you still have your old tap or ballet shoes hidden away?

8. CHINESE RIBBONS: With the music on, give your grandchildren colourful ribbons or crepe paper to twirl about as they dance. You can tie the ribbons onto hair elastics and put them around your grandchild's wrists. Watch rhythmic gymnastics on YouTube.

9. MUSIC AND BOOKS: It is hard to remember all of the words to our grandchildren's favourite songs but there are so many children's books that have been written to accompany so many of their favourites.

 FURTHER READING:

Old MacDonald Had A Farm by Child's Play and Adams
Knick Knack Paddywhack by Zelinsky

The Wheels On The Bus: Sing And Move Book by Baby Genius
If You're Happy And You Know It and Here
We Go Looby Loo by Freeman
The Itsy Bitsy Spider And Twinkle Twinkle Little Star by Holm
The Bear Went Over The Mountain by Dorenkamp

More complex Ideas

1. LISTEN: Listen to the music to which your grandchildren listen.

2. MUSIC IS EVERYWHERE: Whether you have a great voice or not introduce your grandchildren to all kinds of different music – jazz, rock, pop, folk, classical. Let them know something about the people who created this music. Consider Karaoke!

3. CONCERTS: Look for concerts for children in your community. Enjoy them together. You will be a big hit if you buy them tickets to a sold out event for their favourite band.

4. BALLET: Take them to the ballet to see *The Nutcracker*! It could be the beginning of a whole new interest.

5. EXERCISES: You may have DVDs that shows a variety of exercises to keep you fit set to music. Perhaps you can do them together?

6. YOGA: There are many DVDs that are accessible and might interest your grand-children. Play calming, meditative music.

FURTHER READING:

Yoga Games For Children: Fun And Fitness With Postures,
Movements And Breath by Bersma & Visscher
Storytime Yoga: Teaching Yoga To Children Through Story by Solis
Yoga Kids: Educating The Whole Child Through Yoga by Wenig
Little Yoga: A Toddler's First Book Of Yoga by Whitford
My Daddy Is A Pretzel: Yoga for Parents and Children by Baptiste

"My granddaughter told me her favourite thing to do with me is to pick out musical instruments and march around with hats on our heads. We have been doing that since she could walk. My best advice is to have 2 baskets filled with all kinds of musical instruments and funny hats and dress up clothes especially shoes. Music and dress up lead to singing and dancing and play acting which stimulates imagination."
JUDI, GRANDMOTHER

@ Hundreds of children's downloadable lyrics and sheet music: www.kiddles.com

MY NANA, CARTER, AGE 8

WORDS, WORDS, WORDS, BOOKS, BOOKS AND MORE BOOKS

Language learning begins the moment a child is born. We communicate with the youngest child when we mimic sounds, gestures and facial expressions. As grandparents we can promote the best possible language, social and literacy skills when we encourage our grandchildren to start conversations and we respond with interest. Children will begin to use a variety of words moving towards talking in short sentences. We can emphasize action and descriptive words and when possible adding gestures that match the words, for example, the word tired followed by a stretch and a yawn. Children's receptive language exceeds their spoken ability so they will understand a great deal more than we might think. With growing multiracial families coming together, we realize that bilingualism is an asset. It is important that we foster multi-language acquisition. Many books are available at local libraries in a wide range of languages.

The Hanen Centre is an excellent resource on language learning for parents and grandparents:

 www.hanen.org/Home.aspx.

There is no greater gift that you can give to your grandchild than a love of the printed word. As well as print versions of books, you may also have an e-reader, a tablet or smart phone and you can download books onto your device. Many of these downloads are now interactive creating even more interest in the printed word. There will be times in the lives of your grandchildren when they experience difficult moments, sometimes with their peers, sometimes with their family and it is important for you to know that there are many wonderful books available that will help you support your grandchild. There are also great books written about grandparents that your grandchildren will love! Here are just some examples but your local library is a storehouse of important resources.

 FURTHER READING:

Grandpa Green by Smith
I Already Knew I Love You by Crystal
How To Babysit A Grandma by Reagan
How To Babysit A Grandpa by Reagan
Silly Frilly Grandma Tillie by Jacobs

My Grandma Could Do Anything by Dilz
Just Grandma And Me by Mayer
Grandma, Grandpa And Me by Mayer
Grandma Kisses by Nelson
Alfie And Grandma by Hughes
Because Your Grandparents Love You by Clements
Time Together Me And Grandma by Catherine
Time Together Me And Grandpa by Catherine

Simple Ideas

"We have just found out that our daughter is pregnant with her first child. I cannot tell you how excited we are! There were many things I wish I had done differently with my own children but now I get a second chance!" MIRIAM, GRANDMOTHER TO BE

1. INFANT/TODDLER BOOKS: Photo albums, both big and small make perfect books for little hands. You can include nature items under plastic pages to make a durable and interesting book for young children.

2. WORDS: The development of language is often supported when we label items in our environments and when we sing and do simple finger plays. Responsive vocalization is not only fun but encourages important interactions between you and your grandchild.

3. WINTER GLOVES: Another use for winter gloves is to place stickers onto each finger and make up a silly rhyme or song or use a favourite book as a theme to create some fun!

4. SIGNING: There are many books now available to teach children how to sign. Even infants are capable of communicating by sign language. An excellent website to help you with basic signs can be found at:

@   www.babysignlanguage.com.

5. LIBRARY VISITS: Use your local library, schedule reading time and look for special events. Many libraries partner with Early Learning Centres and offer sessions where parents/grandparents can come together to enjoy books, music and games.

6. BOOK STORE: A local children's bookstore can be a very special place for you and your grandchild. Creating excitement about purchasing a new book, continuing the next book in a series etc. is one of the most important things you can do. Make reading fun! Every time you buy a new book for your grandchild, date it and add a message. These will be a treasure in the years to come.

7. READ, READ AND READ SOME MORE: Read in a tent, under the table, in the bath. Read everything - books, newspaper clippings, cartoons, magazines, cereal boxes – just keep reading!

8. FAVOURITE BOOKS: Be prepared to read favourite books over and over and over again. Young children never seem to tire of their favourites. If a child has a favourite book – *Clifford the Big Red Dog* for example, you might create a story bag that has Clifford items in it – a Clifford pencil, stickers, a note pad with Clifford on it, a stuffed Clifford the dog etc.

9. ANIMAL FABLES: Explain that fables are stories that most often include animals that speak.

 FURTHER READING:

Aesop's Fables by Aesop
Aesop's Fables by Cech & Jarrie
Animal Fables From Aesop by McClintock
The Dragon's Tale And Other Aesop Fables
Of The Chinese Zodiac by Demi

10. CRAFTY BOOKS: *The Very Busy Spider* by Eric Carle is a great opportunity to create a web made from yarn. You could give your grandchild pieces of wool and ask them to place the wool in the glue. They can wind the yarn over a piece of wax paper until they have created their masterpiece. Let dry and lift off the waxed paper and hang. You might find a small plastic spider at the dollar store to add.

11. NAMES: Nothing is more special than the name of your grandchild. Help them identify the letters of their name in magazines, newspapers, travel brochures etc. Use wonderful smelly or brilliantly coloured markers to do this. As they are able, look for words they will recognize in print.

12. MAKE A BIRTH BOOK: You may want to create a birth book for your grand-child or a diorama that includes the birth bracelet, a lock of their hair, the card from their incubator, first photo, an ultrasound photo, measurements — weight height etc. This can also be created electronically as well.

13. FUN RHYMES: There are many simple rhymes that encourage an active child to keep moving and some of these rhymes have been made into books! An example:

> Teddy Bear Teddy Bear turn around
> Teddy Bear Teddy Bear touch the ground
> Teddy Bear Teddy Bear touch your shoe
> Teddy Bear Teddy Bear that will do.

You can change the words to encourage more fun and careful listening.
Another favourite:

> See the sleeping bunnies til it's nearly noon
> (here the child drops to the floor)
> Come let us wake them and sing a merry tune
> Oh so still, are they ill?
> Wake up bunnies, hop hop hop
> (here the child leaps up and hops about)
> Wake up bunnies, hop and stop

More favourites:

What can you do Punchinello, funny fellow
What can you do Punchinello, funny fellow funny you?
(the child creates a funny action)
We can do it too Punchinello funny fellow
(you repeat what the child has done)
We can do it too Punchinello funny you.

More complex Ideas

1. NOT SURE?: If you are not sure of your grandchild's reading level a local librarian or book store owner will be more than happy to help. They will also be able to alert you to popular authors or book events coming to your city.

2. AUDIO BOOKS: There are a great many books that will be fun to listen to on drives in the car or in your home.

3. WRITE: Write letters together and send emails to far away relatives and friends. Make mystery letters by writing out a young child's dictation, cut it into pieces, pop it into an envelope and send it by mail to a friend or family member or to themselves to be opened when they are home.

4. HAPPY LETTERS: Slip a happy letter into your grandchildren's take home bags to be opened when they get home. Talk about the fun you had together, how proud you are of them, a major accomplishment or just how much you love them etc.

5. STORY BAGS: You can place a range of objects in the bag dependent on your grandchild's age and ask them to put their hand in the bag without looking and pull out an object. Have them begin a story with that prop then off they go, each time they pull out an object the story changes direction. Encourage their imaginative thoughts and ideas.

6. MAGNETIC LETTERS: Magnetic letters that stick to any magnetic surface are great fun for young children as they put the letters together to make their name.

For older children you could leave a message on the refrigerator upon their arrival that spells out one of the fun things that you are going to do together on their visit.

7. ABC: Many children are able to sing the ABC song but their true understanding of letters will come much later. Begin by helping them to identify the letters in their own name. Ninety five percent of what children will read will be in lower case so begin to identify those letters first – capital for the first letter of their name then lower case after that.

8. ALPHABET BOOKS: Some children may be inspired to create their own ABC book by drawing or cutting out pictures for their own alphabet book. You can help them make an interesting book cover for their book using contact paper and their decorations. You may want to read some alphabet books to your grandchildren before hand.

 FURTHER READING:

Astounding ABC by Aga Khan Museum
My First ABC by Corrigan
The Alphabet Book by P.D. Eastman
A B See by Doyle
Z Is For Zamboni: A Hockey Alphabet by Napier and Rose
M Is For Maple by Ulmer and Rose
M Is For Mountie: A Royal Canadian Mounted
Police Alphabet by Horvath and Bennett
C Is For Chinook: An Alberta Alphabet by Welykochy and Bennett
P Is For Puffin: A Newfoundland and Labrador
Alphabet by Skirving and Archibald
M Is For Meow: A Cat Alphabet by Wilbur
S Is For S'mores: A Camping Alphabet by James and Judge

9. STORYTELLING: Storytelling can be great fun. Telling stories using props and a variety of voices is always entertaining. Personalize the stories by using family names.

10. LIBRARY STORIES ONLINE: Many libraries and other reading organizations have phone lines and online opportunities where you can request and listen or view a story.

11. WHAT ARE THEIR INTERESTS?: A way to attract children to books is to be aware of their interests. Choose books both fiction and non-fiction that compliment and expand on this interest. Talk about the characters, what do you think will happen next, discussing the order of events when the book has been read etc.

12. GETTING STUCK: When children read and make an error or pause because they are not sure of the word, stop and give them time to try and decipher the word. Help them by encouraging them to make the sound of the first letter, let them make a guess but don't wait so long that they get frustrated before you help them with the word.

13. READING MORE: As children become more able to decipher words, encourage them to read more on their own. If they tire easily – you read one page and they read the next.

14. HOMEWORK HELP: There are times when a grandparent is more able to get their grandchild to focus on their homework. In many households with so many demands on parents, homework at times escalates into homework wars! Patience is something most grandparents have in abundance!

15. SCRABBLE: Older children will enjoy games like scrabble but if you have a board and there are letters that are missing, use those letters to create words or sorting and matching the letters that are the same.

16. FAMILY CROSSWORD: Create a simple crossword puzzle using the names of members of your family.

17. BOOK CLUB: As your grandchildren get older and start reading more demanding material, you might want to start a book club where they recommend books for you to read and for you to do the same. When you come together you can discuss and analyze the plot, characters, storyline etc.

18. LETTERS BACK TO YOU: You might consider giving your grandchildren self addressed envelopes to send back to you filled with their latest drawings or important news.

19. CALLING CARDS: Give grandchildren calling cards so they can stay in touch and share among other things what they are reading.

20. MAGAZINES: Give a magazine subscription such as Chirp, Babybug, Ladybug, Chickadee, Ranger Rick, National Geographic Kids, Sports Illustrated Kids, Spider.

21. JOKES: As children grow their understanding of humour increases. Even if they don't get the punch line they often will string words together, pause and then burst out laughing. This is a great opportunity to experiment with language. Knock Knock Jokes are very popular with young children.

 FURTHER READING:

> *Laugh Out Loud Jokes For Kids by Elliott*
> *Jokelopedia: 3rd Edition. The Biggest Best Silliest*
> *Dumbest Joke Book Ever by Wright et al.*
> *Just Joking: 300 Hilarious Jokes, Tricky Tongue Twisters,*
> *and Ridiculous Riddles by National Geographic Kids*
> *The Everything Kids' Giant Book of Jokes, Riddles*
> *and Brain Teasers by Dahl et al.*

22. ALERTS: Write simple words and reminders on wipe off boards.

23. CREATE AN ALL ABOUT ME BOOK: You can find templates online or you can use construction paper or print off a page of the book with corresponding pictures from clip art etc. and have the children fill in the blanks in the book you create together. Listening carefully to their ideas may also help you to understand issues they may be facing or troubling feelings. Ideas for the pages of your book:

> *My family...*
> *My favourite colour...*
> *My favourite toys...*
> *My favourite foods...*
> *My favourite books...*
> *My favourite piece of clothing...*
> *Things I like to do with my friends...*
> *I have fun when....*
> *I get angry when....*

I feel sad when....
I feel afraid when....
I am happy when....
When I grow up...

You can create a collage for the last page of the book of all of their favourite things.

"Books were like treasures to me. My grandmother never arrived at our house that she didn't bring me a book. They were always wrapped in fancy paper and I was always so excited to see what she had brought. Today I am an author and I know that I owe my grandmother an incredible debt." NICOLE, GRANDDAUGHTER

24. YOU BOOK: **Why not create a book for your grandchild that is all about you! Include** old photos especially those photos that represent you when you were their age.

25. MEMORIES OF MY GRANDCHILD: Create your own journal or book about the things you remember most about your grandchild. You might write in this journal several times a year or even just once on their birthday. Talk about their interests, funny anecdotes that you can remember and other memorable moments. You might share this on a special occasion such as leaving home for college or university when they will miss their family the most.

26. LETTERS: Write letters to your grandchildren even before they are born and throughout their lives. Use snail mail to send letters. There is no better feeling than getting your own mail.

27. MAKE LISTS: Make all kinds of list, shopping, ideas for menus, weird words.

28. TIME CAPSULE: Gathering together some favourite things, lists of best books ever and bury them in a secret spot. Date the container and make a plan as to when you want to open this up again.

29. SUMMER FUN: Recall the fun things that happened, for example, over the summer. Arrange photos or create a power point with photos of all your adventures. It can be viewed over and over again.

30. PLAY GAMES: Play Hangman, Concentration, simple word games.

31. PLAY CHARADES: For young children you might print off a picture of the charade but older children may be able to read the instructions. Some examples — eat a banana, mow the lawn, change a diaper, make yourself a sandwich, make a bed, cut someone's hair, take a huge dog for a walk, get a home run.

32. AUTOGRAPH BOOK: Your grandchildren could create an autograph book and collect signatures of friends, relatives and famous people.

33. CHECK OUT THE WEATHER: In the newspaper or online find out the city temperatures and weather where your relatives live.

34. CARTOONS: Read cartoons together, create your own.

35. WHICH ONE IS DIFFERENT?: Ask your grandchild which one doesn't belong – apple, banana, dog?

36. RHYMING: Play the rhyming game – how many words can they think of that rhyme with their name. Otherwise, hat is always a good one to start with if their name is a tricky one. Cut out pictures from magazines of words that rhyme. This is a good time to introduce poetry.

 FURTHER READING:

> *Any Dr. Seuss Book*
> *The Random House Book Of Poetry And Read Aloud*
> *Rhymes For The Very Young by Prelutsky*
> *Sing A Song Of Popcorn by De Regniers*
> *Hip Hop Speaks To Children: A Celebration of*
> *Poetry With A Beat by Giovanni*
> *National Geographic Book Of Animal Poetry by Lewis*
> *Alligator Pie, Garbage Delight, Willoughby Wallaby Woo by Lee*
> *Un Deux Trois: First French Rhymes by Dunn and Aggs*
> *Chinese And English Nursery Rhymes: Share And Sing in Two*
> *Languages With Audio CD by Wu and Dutcher. Books are also*
> *available for those interested in Korean and Japanese Rhymes*

37. PROVERBS: How many proverbs or sayings can you come up with that have their roots in nature – "light as a feather", "a rolling stone gathers no moss', "the calm before the storm", "sly as a fox", "can't see the forest for the trees", "every cloud has a silver lining". Can you think of others?

@ Lots of ideas for children's magazines: www.cricketmag.com

@ Find out the latest information on children's books at:
www.childrensbook.about.com

"When I think of my two grandmothers, I think of strong women. The traditions, the food and the love that they shared have shaped the woman I have become." KATE, GRANDDAUGHTER

"Grandparents and grandchildren are destined to love each other. Grandchildren come into grandparents' lives at a time when they are free to simply love and enjoy them; they have the wisdom of knowing it all turns out in the end. For children, grandparents can be a mirror of truth in an often difficult world; grandparents allow kids to see themselves reflected as they truly are - awe-inspiring, loved, valued, and perfect." ERIN, DAUGHTER

MY GRAMPS, JACK, AGE 4

MATH AND SCIENCE

Children begin to develop math skills early in infancy. They are beginning to understand spatial relationships when they maneuver themselves into position to grab a toy. When toddlers climb, crawl and walk over, under and around objects and stack their rings and blocks, they discover more about the shape and size of the world in which they live. A child learns by observing, investigating, doing, listening, talking, reflecting, reasoning, interacting, discussing, and applying! Children make discoveries when they explore and manipulate themselves and the materials around them. They learn best when manipulating concrete materials that are familiar and meaningful to them – real objects such as pairing socks out of the dryer, sorting a collection of keys or shells or containers. While it is important for children to learn to count and to read and write numerals, a more important objective is for the child to construct the *mental structure of number* – to truly understand the "numberness of number". Through their observations, they can explore, predict, and test information and ideas. The children will learn that there are many ways to approach and solve problems. This promotes cognitive flexibility and respect for diversity of thought. As your grandchildren grapple with challenging problems, they learn the value of perseverance and the benefit of effort. As they experience success their self confidence grows. Mistakes should be treated as opportunities for learning. The internalization of math concepts and development of language skills go hand in hand. Grandparents can encourage this development by asking open ended questions that ask for more information or explanation:

What do you think will happen next?
What do you think the next colour will be?

Which one do you think weighs the most?
How many do you think are in this container?
What's wrong with my counting?

Young children are naturally curious about the world around them. Involvement in science and technology will help and encourage children to appreciate the beauty and value of their natural environment, to respect all living things, and to develop the attitudes, skills, and knowledge required to make informed decisions. Through hands on experiences, young children are capable of understanding scientific concepts and making observations and predictions that encourage the development of critical thinking skills. An early understanding of animals, plants, weather and the physical environment in which they live are important learning opportunities. This learning also promotes increased discussion and an expanding vocabulary.

"My grandmother was a retired teacher and she never missed an opportunity to link math and science to just about everything! Today I teach Science to high school kids and I hope I can help them feel as excited about learning as my grandmother did! Big shoes to fill!" SEAN, GRANDSON

Simple Ideas

1. BLOCKS: Use a variety of sponges as blocks cut into shapes. Another inexpensive idea is to use old cereal, cracker or other food boxes and crumple newspaper inside to make them sturdy. Seal off with duct tape and you have an interesting set of blocks. You can add another element by drawing and cutting and pasting onto the blocks; a city scape – the library, the market, the garage, the fire station etc.

2. PURCHASED BLOCKS: There are many open ended types of block type materials that will provide hours of fun – Duplo, Lego, K'Nex, Meccano, Quadro, Stickle Bricks, Tinker Toys, Wooden Blocks etc.

4. BUBBLES: Bubbles are always a favourite activity. Which wands make the best bubbles? What happens when you blow bubbles in the winter?

5. OIL AND WATER: Fill an ice cube tray with water and put a drop of different food colouring into each section. Using a tray, pour a small amount of olive oil or vegetable oil on the tray. Pop out the ice cubes and enjoy moving them around the tray. An interesting experiment that is perfect for little fingers, especially on a really hot day.

6. TODDLERS LOVE TO PUSH AND PULL: Use paper towel rolls and punch a hole in the end of each one and tie them together using yarn. Attach a long piece of yarn for the handle. They can paint them as well.

7. TODDLER FUN: Turn a colander upside down and give toddlers thin straws or pipe cleaners to push into the holes. A great fine motor activity.

8. BALLS AND TUBES: Even the youngest child will be enamoured by what happens to the ball when it is put into a tube! Collect tubes in a variety of sizes and an assortment of attention-grabbing balls.

9. SINK AND FLOAT: Use a baby bath tub and fill it with a variety of objects, some that will float and some that will sink. Ask them to predict what they think will happen. You may want to create some paper boats to try.

10. MAGNIFYING GLASS: Use a variety of magnifiers and explore! If you wear glasses, explain how they help you to see.

11. MAGNET FUN: A simple magnetic experience is to start with a metal baking tray. Glue magnets on the bottom of objects such as small cars, left over puzzle pieces and place them on the tray. Run the magnet under the tray and watch them move. Magnetic objects are also available in many toy stores.

12. WHAT STICKS?: Use a variety of different magnets and do a walk about to see what sticks and what does not. You might gather a number of household objects and have your grandchild predict whether it will stick to the magnet or not.

13. MAGNETIC LETTERS AND NUMBERS: Magnetic numbers and letters can be purchased and placed on your refrigerator or dishwasher. Let your grandchild explore.

14. COLOURS: There are so many ways to identify colours! Try labelling the colour of their clothes, the fruits and vegetables they are eating, the colour of your car etc. etc.

15. STRINGING COLOURS: Use colourful beads and matching coloured shoelaces. See if your grandchild can string all the red beads on the red shoelace etc.

16. PAPER PLATE MATCH: Lay out some paper plates and put a different colour of Duplo on each plate. See if your grandchild can match the colour by filling up each paper plate with more Duplo of the same colour.

17. SORTERS: Look for containers that are divided into sections for children to sort their treasures – washed out egg cartons, fishing tackle boxes, plastic jewellery containers, fruit and vegetable trays, muffin tins, ice cube trays etc.

18. SORTING BUTTONS: Young children will want to explore a large collection of buttons but older children may be engaged in placing all the same colour buttons in a compartment of a plastic fruit tray or muffin tin. Buttons should be large for young children to prevent choking issues.

19. SHAPES: Look for shapes in their everyday environment – street signs, traffic lights, bowls etc. You may want to purchase a shape sorter to expand on this concept.

20. MATCHING GAMES: Matching games are great ways for children to develop early math skills. There are so many ways to make these types of games with inexpensive materials. For example, save the lids off frozen juice containers or water bottle tops and purchase a double set of stickers. Place the stickers on the juice lids and have your grandchildren find the match.

21. POM POM MATCH: You need a paper egg carton, small tongs and small pom poms in four colours. Paint or use markers to colour the insides of all the sections of the egg carton. Put all the pom poms in a large Ziploc bag along with the tongs. Encourage your grandchild to use the tongs to place the same colour pom pom into the correct egg section. This experience also supports their fine motor skills. Little ones will just have fun putting the pom poms into the carton or more likely, throwing them into the air.

22. NOTE PADS: Many note pads now come in a wide range of choices in interesting shapes – school buses, apples, running shoes etc. Put duplicate stickers on the sheets and see if your grandchild can find the match.

23. PAIR IT UP: When travelling pick up doubles of postcards and upon your return mix them all together and see if your grandchild can find the matching pair.

24. WRAPPING PAPER MATCH: Most wrapping paper has a repeated pattern. Cut up the objects in the patterns and see if your grandchild can find the match.

25. MATCHING CARD BINGO: Depending on your grandchild's skill level, create a simple Bingo card and use playing cards to play the game. Children search for the matching card, place it on top of the same card and when their card is full they shout BINGO!

26. STAMPS: Purchase a few animal stamps or letter and number stamps and prepare "which one is different cards" by using index cards or tag board and

for example, stamping three Brontosaurus and one Stegosaurus or a more difficult challenge might be stamping four letters facing one direction and one the opposite way. If you laminate the cards they can be used over and over. Your grandchild just circles the one that is different with a dry erase marker and they can be wiped off to be used again. These cards can also be made using a package of interesting stickers.

27. SERIATION: This is when children learn about sizes — big, bigger, biggest; small, medium, large. Use dollar store boxes that fit inside each other for fancy blocks and perfect for stacking for young children. Matryoshka dolls are a perfect example of seriation or you can create your own examples.

28. COLLECTIONS: Many children are very keen on finding, organizing and keeping collections over time. Some collections might include keys, bottle caps, buttons, coins, marbles, postcards, rocks, shells, stamps, coloured Popsicle sticks, coloured clothes pins, straws, coloured paper clips, stickers etc. Sorting, organizing and building with their collections can provide hours of fun. Find great see-through containers for easy access in which to keep them all. If you have a collection this is the perfect time to share yours with them!

29. RAMPS: Create ramps with long boards or blocks. Raise and lower the height of the ramps and predict how far your wheeled vehicles will travel.

30. RACING TRACK: Cut a pool noodle in half and create a racing track for small cars or marbles. Estimate how far they will go.

"Growing up my idol and biggest fan was my Grandpa. He was an amazing person and I learned a great deal from him during his healthier years. I spent many hours helping him in the basement workshop with whatever he was doing. He was very skilled at working with his hands for construction and carpentry and actually built his own house." MICHAEL, GRANDSON.

MY NANA, MADDEN, AGE 4

More complex Ideas

1. PAINT CHIPS: If you are visiting your local paint store, pick up some of the paint chips and cut them into pieces. Can your grandchild put them in order from darkest to lightest?

2. WOODWORKING: A great activity to do outside since it does create a lot of great sounds. Visit your local lumberyard and ask for scraps. Help your grandchild learn how to safely use real tools, many of which now come in smaller sizes for little hands. Also provide lots of glue!

3. TOOLS: Learn how to use construction tools – try hammering nails in then using a claw hammer to remove them. Build something together – a Little Library or a bird house. For little hands try hammering golf tees into cardboard boxes or another sturdy malleable product.

4. RESOURCES: A visit to the plumbing section of a hardware store provides all kinds of great loose parts for construction – PVC tubing, pipe fittings, clear tubing for running water experiments etc.

5. DETECTIVE WORK: Take apart old appliances with lots of supervision!

6. PATTERNS: The ability to reproduce and create patterns is an early math skill. Help them find patterns in the world around them first (on their shirts, wallpaper, wrapping paper etc). Almost any set of objects around the house can be used to create a simple alternating pattern – spoon, fork, spoon, fork etc. Children can then begin to create their own patterns. You can also help reinforce this skill by creating patterning cards with interesting stickers.

7. PATTERN BEADING: Provide your grandchild with beads and see if he or she can thread a pattern on a shoelace.

8. CLAP AND TAP: Create patterns with your hands by a simple clap then tap your knees. Can your grandchild mimic your actions? Vary the pattern and have your grandchild create patterns for you to follow.

9. STATIC ELECTRICITY: On a dry day when you can generate the most static electricity, blow up balloons and have your grandchild try rubbing them in his or her hair. What happens? Try out a variety of other objects to see if they will stick to the balloon – scarves, combs, paper etc.

10. NUMBERS: Numbers are everywhere! Have a search and find around the house – how many steps to the basement, number of window and doors in the house, and in your neighbourhood look for numbers on the houses and license plates etc.

11. MEASUREMENT: Measurement develops children's understanding of the concepts of length, height, weight, capacity, temperature, time and money. How many different ways can you measure?

12. MEASURE UP: Find a suitable place to record how your grandchild grows over the years.

13. MEASURING CUPS AND SPOONS: Use fun measuring cups and spoons to explore water or to be used in food preparation.

14. WEIGH IT UP: Children may be interested in using a scale to weigh themselves. What else can they weigh? Make a guessing game out of this experience.

15. CALENDARS: Use calendars to mark special events.

16. TIME: Look at the variety of ways in which we tell time such as wrist watches, clocks on TVs or microwaves, clocks on the phone, in the car etc. Help your grand-child learn time, first in simple ways talking about the big and little hand on the clock and then in a digital format.

17. WEATHER CHECK: Check the thermometer both indoors and out.

18. GLOBE: An interesting piece of equipment for an inquisitive mind.

19. SECRET CODES: A great idea for keeping and uncovering secrets. Use Hieroglyphic images to create a code. Use sign language for letters to spell out words. Hide clues to help find the answers.

20. FULL OF HOT AIR: Use straws and ping pong balls and try to blow them off a table.

21. COINS: Use coins from your travels to talk about money around the world.

22. NUMBERS: Use playdough to roll out numbers, perhaps the number that represents how old your grandchild is?

 FURTHER READING:

Five Little Penguins Slipping On The Ice by Metzger and Bryant
Monster Math by Miranda
The Jelly Bean Fun Book by Caucilli
Ten Black Dots by Crew
The Cheerio Counting Book by McGrath
Ten Little Fish by Wood
Each Orange Had 8 Slices by Giganti
Three Little Pigs, Three Bears, Three Billy Goats Gruff
Exploring Kitchen Science: 40+ Delicious Discoveries by Exploratorium
Five Little Ducks by Weidner
10 Little Monkeys Jumping On The Bed by Kubler and Freeman

This Old Man by Jones
One Light, One Sun by Raffi
The Caribbean Counting Book by Charles and Arenson

@ www.education.com/activity/preschool/math/

@ www.pbs.org/parents/education/math/activities/baby-toddler/

@ www.teachpreschoolscience.com/index

@ www.pbs.org/parents/education/science/activities/babies-toddlers/

@ www.pinterest.com/search/pins/?q=science%20for%20preschoolers

PINK NANA AND GRAMPA, BELLA, AGE 3

WHIZ KID TECHNOLOGY

Technology is an inescapable part of our modern culture but the number of hours children, both young and old, spend in front of a screen is a growing concern. The use of the television and the Internet in the home is having a dramatic impact on physical activity, rising health concerns and our connection with the natural world. TVs and DVDs are often used to entertain children as parents cope with their busy lives. Experts often recommend that there should be no screen time for children under two and limited to one hour for children 2-5 years yet we know that more than 90% of children begin watching TV before the age of two. Despite this we know that good programming – think Sesame Street – has the ability to teach our grandchildren important values and life lessons as well as helping children share cultural experiences and develop critical thinking skills about society and the world. Hand held devises are everywhere – you can see children using them in restaurants, on long car rides, just about anywhere. It is easy for us to be overwhelmed with the remarkable array of games for our iPhones, iPads, tablets, notebooks etc. For example, one visit to the Apple Store will demonstrate how many games and programs are available for even the youngest children. Best advice is to take a look at the programs to find the ones that you think are the best fit for your grandchild. Many of these apps are available at no cost.

@ http://store.apple.com/ca.

In addition, you must always take into account the preferences of your grandchild's parents. Some parents do not want any screen time interaction, while others embrace technology for their children wholeheartedly. As in all things related to the grandparenting role, you must follow the lead of your children's wishes. At the end of the day, balance is what we are looking for! Given that your grandchildren may know more about technology than you do, it is a great opportunity for them to teach you what they know!

"I can't tell you how many phone calls and visits to my Grandmothers I have made to help her with her "gadgets" as she likes to call them. There are times when it drives me crazy but I have to say that we laugh together a lot in this process. She always promises me that she won't call again but...." ALEX, GRANDSON

Simple Ideas

"Going through old family photos gave me a better understanding of my relationship with my papa. He truly loved his grandkids and made the most of every moment with them. Every photo he was in, he looked happy to be around his family. He also loved playing Batman with me and we would run around the streets wearing Batman masks!" MIKEY, GRANDSON.

1. CAMERA PUZZLES: Take a photo of your grandchild and glue it onto stiff cardboard and cut it into a number of pieces depending on their skill level for them to put back together.

2. PHOTO MEMORIES: One mother I know takes her children to the same spot in a park and takes a photo of her children every month. This would be a wonderful keepsake as your grandchildren age.

3. KEEP ACTIVE: Nintendo's Wii video game console that encourages a number of interactive experiences will keep everyone active.

4. TELEVISION USE: At the end of the day when you may need a break from your active grandchild an educational television show may be just what you need. There are also many suitable DVDs that you could also show at this time. Review guides to ensure that they are age appropriate. This is also an opportunity for you to discuss together what they are watching.

5. COOKIE MAKING USING THE INTERNET: There are a number of simple cooking recipes for cookies and other fun goodies to eat that can be found on the internet. This visual representation makes it easy to cook up a storm. Here is a great website:

@ grandparents.about.com/od/cookingwithgrandkids/tp/CookieFavorites

6. SOCIAL NETWORKING: There are many ways to connect with your grandchildren by texting, learning how to use Twitter, creating your own Facebook page and sharing your favourite YouTube videos.

"One experience I want to share is the value of today's technology. I FaceTime with my granddaughters a few times a week. Hannah, my youngest granddaughter just turned one and I got to see her eating her birthday cake with cake all over her face and hair; she even tried to give me a bite through the screen! She started walking a few days later and my son FaceTimed me to show me her first steps. It is the best thing next to being there. Hannah often pushes her sisters away if they try to take away our FaceTime!" MONIQUE, GRAND-MERE

More complex Ideas

1. BE A PHOTOGRAPHER: There is no question that a picture is worth a thousand words and this is never more apparent than when young children are involved. We live in a visual world. Cameras are everywhere – in all sizes and shapes, on smart phones and even underwater! The camera allows your grandchild an opportunity to make ideas visible and to help your grandchild explore and really examine the world around them. It is also a tool that can record the same place or subject over time allowing children to revisit their ideas over and over again. Photos of the first flower of spring, a rainfall or snowflakes falling provides ample opportunity to develop their language skills as they discuss their pictures with you. You may be setting the stage for a lifelong passion for taking photographs. Visit the library and look at books of famous photographers such as Ansel Adams, Paul Weston, Alfred Steiglitz, Brian Adams and Annie Liebowitz.

2. PLAN A MOVIE NIGHT: Pick a favourite movie or one just out and watch the movie with all the trimmings – popcorn and your best snacks, pillows and blankets!

3. INSTAGRAM: Create an Instagram account for just you and your grandchildren.

4. REAL TIME: Play games on the computer in real time on devises such as Xbox and PlayStation.

5. GAMING: Many grandchildren will be gaming at some point either on their own smartphones or on consoles such as Nintendo, Xbox or PlayStation. Make sure how much time can be spent on this is discussed well in advance. A reminder again to be careful about buying any games for these devices without speaking to the parents first.

6. YOUR COMPUTER: Make sure that you have backed up all your important information before you let your grandchildren use your computer. Try downloading many of the free games that are available onto your computer and have them ready for your grandchildren when they visit. Try them out first to make sure they are appropriate.

7. FOLDERS ON YOUR COMPUTER: You may want to download all of the pictures that you take with your grandchildren and put them into files with their names on it. This way they can access their own file and relive many of the fun experiences you have had together.

8. CHARGERS: You may want to mark your charging cords with marker so you can easily identify them to keep your cords separate from any your grandchild might bring over.

9. LIVE AWAY GRANNYS AND GRAMPAS: When you are separated from your grandchildren, emails, text messages, Skype, FaceTime and Facebook allow you opportunities to stay in touch with each other. Nothing is more fun than receiving a letter from Granny and Grampa in the mailbox!

10. A SURPRISE: A great deal of excitement will be generated when you send your grandchild a surprise package through the mail that includes a memory stick filled with fun things you have been doing. You could also send an empty one for your grandchild to fill up. It is even more wonderful when it is unexpected!

11. SKYVIEW: Sky View is a free app that brings stargazing to everyone, and it's free. You simply point your iPhone, iPad, or iPod at the sky to identify stars, constellations, and satellites. Perfect for a warm summer night together.

12. CALENDAR: Create an online family calendar everyone can access. This will help you keep track of upcoming events that you won't want to miss.

13. WEBSITE: Create your own family website using free sites that help you get started for example:

 www.webs.com, www.wix.com, www.wordpress.com

14. LONG DISTANT CONNECTIONS: iPad fun! This example below illustrates how this grandfather stays in touch:

"While in Hilton Head, Papa sends our granddaughter animal photos almost every day from his iPad and she and her mom open them together and mom teaches her the sound the animal makes. Then they call us together on FaceTime and our granddaughter sometimes repeats what she's learned!" HEATHER, GRANNY

15. MAPPING WITH TECHNOLOGY: Older children will be interested in using GPS systems to locate familiar landmarks and even their own homes with Google Earth. It's also a great way to take a new and interesting look at your home.

FURTHER READING:

Map and Mapping by Taylor
Follow That Map A First Book of Mapping Skills by Ritchie
Mapping Penny's World by Leedy

 SAFE TECHNOLOGY

The Internet is an incredible resource for children! As the technology revolution has exploded, it has become more and more an integral part of all of our lives. It will be important to create some ground rules in your home that reflect the parent's position on the use of the computer, cell phones and other technology. Parents and grandparents may be anxious about the quality of television programs but there are many shows that the whole family can watch together. Check TV listings and program reviews to find programs that are developmentally appropriate and reinforce your family values. You may also create rules - there will be no TV during meals or when doing homework. It is also important to reduce the risks that children may be exposed to when they are online. Many Internet providers offer parent control options to restrict certain adult content and block inappropriate sites. It is vital to speak to your grandchildren about your concerns and insist that they not give out personal information such as their password, name, age, address, telephone number, school etc. or connect to any pop-up ads, buy things online or download software without your approval. Posting of pictures online should also be discussed. You may want to set up your computer or their devices in an area where you can monitor their activities. With older grandchildren a growing concern is when the Internet, cell phones or other devices are used to send or post text or images that are hurtful to others. Unlike physical bullying, with Cyberbullying the person can remain virtually anonymous. Your grandchildren should feel comfortable coming to you if they experience something online that raises a red flag or makes them feel uncomfortable.

MY PAPA, CARTER, AGE 8

RAINY DAY ACTIVITIES

Rainy days can present all kinds of issues, particularly when special plans have to be put aside. Having back up ideas may help ease the pain – always have a backup plan!

Simple Ideas

1. GO OUT: With the proper gear, this can be fun experience. Look for critters outside – worms peaking out of the grass, spider webs covered in rain, check out the rain drops on plants, look for rainbows and most importantly jump in the puddles!

2. RAINY DAY SUITCASE: Small, easy to manage suitcases can be filled with all kinds of interesting props and materials. This suitcase might be saved for just this occasion filled with interesting dress up clothes, jewelry, fancy hats, purses, computer bags, scarves, boas, pirate hats, eye patches, chef hat etc. Anything that your grandchildren usually doesn't have access to.

 ## FURTHER READING:

Stop! There's A Snake In Your Suitcase by Frost & Chambers
Sammy's Suitcase by Rojany Buccieri, Foster & Yoshikawa
Silly Milly & The Mysterious Suitcase by Lewison and Westcott
Grandma's Suitcase. Where A Kid Can Always Find A Surprise! By Dyan

3. COZY SPACE: Try something different by setting up a blanket under a table; add some pillows and some stuffed animals. Crawl under and perhaps bring some snacks with you. Read some books while you are there!

4. INSIDE PICNIC: You may spread out a blanket and sit on the floor while eating your picnic lunch.

5. OLD PHOTO ALBUMS: This might be a perfect day to bring out old photo albums and show them to your grandchild. Even better if you have pictures of you when you were their age!

6. CRAYOLA WINDOW MARKERS: A perfect idea for a rainy day and these markers are easily removed.

7. DRIED FLOWERS: Press flowers that you have picked mid-morning when the dew is off them in heavy books and on a rainy day pull them out. Dried flowers are beautiful additions to homemade greeting cards, place cards or thank you notes.

8. ROAD WORKS: Using masking tape, create roads on the floor for wheeled vehicles.

9. SCAVENGER HUNT: A perfect day to create some fun inside the house. Hide some treasures and for young children to be successful let the prizes poke out of their hiding place. With older children written clues will increase the suspense.

10. CUT AND PASTE: If you keep old magazines about these are great for creating collages of their latest interests – jungle animals, food they would like to eat, cars they would like to ride in etc.

More complex Ideas

1. WRITER'S SUITCASE: Create a writer's box by collecting for example, smelly markers, calligraphy pens, thin markers, fancy pencils, pencil sharpener, erasers, pencil crayons, crayons, charcoal, oil pastels, ballpoint pens, stapler, staples, clipboard, container of stickers, coloured paper, index cards, tag board, graph paper, chart paper, books made from construction paper with white paper inside, envelopes, chalkboards, eraser, chalk, magic slates, magnetic board, hole punch, paper clips,

paper fasteners, pencil boxes, Chinese brushes, stamps, stamp pads, rulers, scissors. Save this suitcase for rainy days only.

2. DEAR DIARY: A rainy day may be a great time to talk about personal writing. Some older children might enjoy making their own diary and writing down their thoughts and feelings. Covers can be made from Batik, Marbled Paper or Tie Dying. More and more programs are available for bookmaking on the internet

3. RAIN STICK: Your grandchild might want to decorate a paper towel roll to create a spectacular rain stick. When done, tightly seal off one end of the paper towel tightly with cloth and masking tape or crazy glue. Pour in small stones and seal closed. Listen to the music the stones makes. Traditionally made from a dried cactus, the rain stick would have the spines from the cactus inserted like nails so that the pebbles would jump through the stick. Originally created by the Aztecs it was thought that the movement of the stick that sounds like water would bring on the rain.

4. RAINY DAY ART: Watercolours are good for pastel colours and washes. Your grandchildren can paint their pictures and then put them outside in the rain to see what happens. You can also sprinkle on salt while the picture is still wet. When the salt dries, it will sparkle.

5. PAINTING IN THE RAIN: When the rain is drizzling and no lighting is insight, take some watercolour paints and some chalk and decorate the sidewalk. What happens to the paint and chalk when the rain falls on it?

6. PUDDLES: With a big rainfall it may be possible to sail some paper boats in some of the larger puddles!

7. BOATS: Nothing is more fun than when it is really really raining than to go outside and block the water to create rivers using rocks and sticks and sail some boats!

8. SING: Good time to sing the "Rain Rain Go Away" song or "It's Raining It's Pouring".

9. MEASURE: Set up a measuring cup or a pail and measure how much rain actually falls? While you are waiting and if it is really raining hard, take out a variety of empty containers, put them upside down and listen to the sound the rain makes splashing off these objects.

FURTHER READING:

The Cat In The Hat by Dr. Seuss
Rain Rain Go Away by Church
Let It Rain by Cocca-Leffler
Cloudy With The Chance of Meatballs by Barrett
Where Did The Rain Puddle Go? by Bently
Rain by Spiers
Taste The Raindrops by Hines
The Rainy Day Puddles by Nakabayashi
Big Rain Coming by Germein

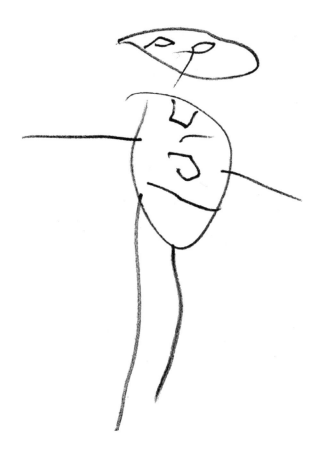

MY GRANDFATHER, SAMIR, AGE 3

GAMES

This is an opportunity to encourage non-competitive games and look for more cooperative approaches to play. This is my favourite poem by the late Shel Silverstein, author of *A Light In the Attic*:

Hug O' War

I will not play at tug o' war
I'd rather play at hug o' war,
Where everyone hugs
Instead of tugs
Where everyone giggles
And rolls on the rug,
Where everyone kisses
And everyone grins
And everyone cuddles
And everyone wins.

Timing and pace are integral to a fun experience. When playing games together you may want to go over the ground rules first so that everyone understands the objective. You may have to alter some games when playing with younger children. Watch to see when your grandchildren are beginning to lose interest or just getting tired. Try to end on a high note.

Simple Ideas

1. DICE: Dice promote number recognition and counting skills – roll away.

2. LOTTO GAMES: Lots of skills are learned when using Lotto Cards.

3. JIGSAW PUZZLES: Pick puzzles that are appropriate for the age and development of your grandchild. There are puzzles for infants with large knobs on the piece for easy handling, all the way up to puzzles with more than 100 pieces. Encourage their transition from simple to more complex puzzles. Monitor those with tiny pieces that might be swallowed by young children.

4. PLAY PICK-UP STICKS: Use shish kabob sticks if you don't have the real thing. Paint the tips for different point values.

5. MARBLES: Marbles are fun to collect because they are all so different. Age old games involve marbles. Other ideas - add long paper tubes from wrapping paper and paper towels etc to create runways for their marbles.

 FURTHER READING:

The Marble Book by Chevat
Imaginative Inventions: The Who, What, Where, When And
Why of Roller Skates, Potato Chips, Marbles And Pie by Harper
Play Marbles by Levine
Arthur Loses His Marbles by Krensky

6. PLAYING CARDS: Cards can be used to create games that promote comparisons, they can be used to count how many cards are red, how many are hearts, how many are face cards etc. Games like Animal Rummy, Snap, Go Fish, Uno, Yahtzee, Crazy Eights or Concentration teach grouping and sorting - basic math skills. Learning how to play Solitaire is an advanced skill but perfect when solo time is a must. Some stores carry blank playing cards and you can create your own symbols. There is always Euchre and Bridge for over achievers not to mention learning how to shuffle!

FURTHER READING:

The Book Of Card Games For Kids by MacColl
The Book of Card Games For Little Kids by MacColl
Card Games For Smart Kids by Golick

"My favourite memories of my grandmother are the times she read to me or just played cards. There is such a different relationship with grandchildren than with your own children. My experience is that they are much more open and feel less inhibited with grandparents." DIANNE, GRANDMOTHER

7. CARD TRICKS: Books are available for you to learn how to trick your grandchildren!

8. JACKS: Bounce the little ball and how many jacks can you pick up before it lands on the ground?

9. RED LIGHT, GREEN LIGHT/WHAT TIME IS IT MR WOLF/RED ROVER/SIMON SAYS: You may remember these but if not, let your grandchildren teach you how to play these games.

10. MUSICAL STATUES: Play the music and when it stops, hold your position without falling over, without laughing etc. Set up your own rules for this one.

11. CLOTHESPINS IN THE BOTTLE: Find a wide mouth plastic container and long clothes pins. Stand over the container and see how many pegs can be dropped in.

12. KIM'S GAME: This simple memory game is great fun. Depending on the age of your grandchild, arrange a variety of easy to identify objects on a tray. Let your grandchild study the tray for a few minutes then cover it with a towel. With younger children you can place just a few objects on the tray, let them look, cover it over and remove one of the items. Can your grandchild guess which one?

13. EASY CATCH: Try cutting out the bottom of a large laundry soap tub, flip it over and try to catch tennis balls.

14. BALLS AND CANS: The cans that tennis balls come in or larger types of cans can be used for the children to try and catch tennis balls.

15. OBSTACLE COURSE: A good way to encourage excellent bicycling skills is to set up an obstacle course. Use old tires, chairs, hoops, ropes, chalk lines etc.

16. HIDE AND SEEK: An age old favourite!!

17. FLEECE BALLS: Balls can be made by wrapping wool around a cardboard circle with the centre cut out. When enough wool is wrapped, a length of wool is tied around the centre and tied off. Remove the cardboard.

18. BALL WALL: Create patterns and targets on the wall with paint or chalk.

19. TARGET PRACTICE: You can cut out shapes in a cardboard box and have your grandchild attempt to toss a bean bag into the hole. You can create an even simpler activity by providing a laundry basket and bean bags. Move the basket further away as their skills improve.

20. NYLON STOCKINGS: A knee high with a tennis ball in the toe and tied off can be bounced on the ground or against the wall. You can also swing this around and toss it some distance. Have your grandchild estimate how far they think they will throw it. Measure it off.

21. BALLOON BATS: Create a "bat" by covering a metal coat hanger bent into a diamond or circle shape, twist the hook of the hanger to form a closed handle. Pull a nylon stocking over the hanger and secure it to the handle with masking tape or tie it off. Use balloons to bat about! (Safety tip: balloons are only safe for young children if they are wrapped inside a nylon stocking to prevent choking). A simpler version is to use paper towel rolls to hit the balloons.

More complex Ideas

1. PANTOMIME: Children in this area may enjoy acting out a Pantomime to a favourite story.

2. LIP SYNCING: Interested children may be interested in putting on a stage performance while lip syncing to their favourite songs.

3. BOARD GAMES: Be on the lookout for board games at garage sales! These games teach all kinds of skills – Monopoly, Boggle, Scrabble, Clue, Checkers, Chess, Bingo, Snakes and Ladders, Twister, Candy Land, Kerplunk, Hungry Hungry Hippos, Spot It, Connect 4, Simon, Operation, Hedbanz, Sorry, Chinese Checkers, Game of Life, Bananagrams, Battleship, Mousetrap, Cribbage, and Spot It. Make a night of it, playing everyone's favourites.

4. DOMINOES: Dominoes are played all around the world and new dominoes have been created with pictures for matching for younger children.

5. BASEBALL/TBALL: Lots of fun can be had in the backyard just throwing the ball around. A trip to see your favourite baseball team could be a great road trip!

 FURTHER READING:

Baseball Bats For Christmas by Kusugak
Curious George At The Baseball Game by Rey
I Spy With My Little Eye: Baseball by Herzog
H Is For Home Run: A Baseball Alphabet Book by Herzog
I Can Play Baseball by Eckart

6. SPORTS: Not just baseball, how about basketball, tennis, skiing, swimming, balloon volleyball, skiing etc. etc. Let's keep moving and watching! Many hours can be spent in a gym, hockey arena or T-ball field! Bring a cushion.

"My son and my dad get along famously because they a share a love for sports. My dad is so proud of him and sure that he could become a professional athlete in any sport, another great thing about being a grandparent! There is no reason to see anything but good and positive in your grandchildren. Everyone has the best grandchildren in the world. Funny how that works!" KARYN, PARENT

7. SKIPPING: There are many skipping chants and children will enjoy seeing how long they can skip without tripping up. What chants do you remember?

8. BALL AGAINST THE WALL: Remember red, white and blue balls and the throwing game against the wall – teach it to your grandchildren.

9. HOOLA HOOPS: A fun activity for grandparents and grandchildren. Twist away!

10. HOP SCOTCH AROUND THE WORLD: Hopscotch is a great way to build healthy bones. As well as using numbers in the squares, try adding colours, shapes, letters, children's names etc. for something new!

11. ROLLER BLADING/IN-LINE SKATING: With the proper safe equipment, roller blading can be a great experience for older children.

12. JUGGLING: A good way to start to learn how to juggle is to use bean bags! Start with one then move on to more. Hold one bean bag in your dominant hand, throw it up in an arch and catch it with your other hand. Pass it back and forth then try reversing your throw then move on to two bean bags!

13. CROQUET/BOULE/BOCHE: These old time games are always fun.

14. LACROSSE: Lacrosse is a Native American game and is a popular team sport that uses a stick with a net at the end and a hard ball. There are many Aboriginal games and resources that can be found on this website:

@ www.ainc-inac.gc.ca/ach/lr/ks/index-eng.asp

15. FRISBEE GAMES: Try playing Frisbee golf. Set up markers that the children can attempt to hit with their throws. With younger children just catching the Frisbee is a major event.

 FURTHER READING:

Andy And His Yellow Frisbee by Thompson
The Wham O Ultimate Frisbee Handbook: Tips And Techniques
For Playing Your Best Ultimate Frisbee by Sach & Copeland
Plastic: Let's Look At Frisbees by Royston

16. CHARADES: This game can be played in small teams or with two people. You make up book titles, songs, movies, a TV show etc. and the other team acts it out without speaking. You can use a timer to help speed the game along. For younger children, pictures can be used that they act out or they might try to act out a nursery rhyme or a story book character. You could download pictures from the Internet, for example, a picture of Clifford the Big Red Dog, show it to your

grandchild and have them act it out for others to guess. Older children will be able to read the clues.

17. PICTIONARY: Older grandchildren can be divided into two small teams and each person on the team chooses a card with a word such as flower and the child goes to the easel and draws the picture until someone guesses.

"I have remarried after divorcing my husband and now the children have 6 pairs of grandparents. I honestly believe that children can never have enough people in their lives who love them dearly. I do everything I can to maintain a positive relationship with my ex-husband and his parents and they are included in all our special events and occasions. I wouldn't have it any other way!" CINZIA, PARENT

"Even though both sets of my children's grandparents are gone now, we never miss an opportunity to laugh at the things we remember - times that make us laugh so hard we cannot catch our breath. We also remember how hard they fought their illnesses without complaint, their countless kindnesses and the deep love they had for all of us. I can only hope that one day my grandchildren will remember me with the same passion and affection." SARA, PARENT

PARTY TIME/FESTIVALS

There are so many festivals and holidays that are celebrated by our diverse culture in our country. We support our grandchildren's understanding of others when we celebrate not only the events that are important to our own faith or family history but to also embrace the cultural events and holidays of our neighbours and fellow citizens. There are many books and resources available for us in our own community that provide us with a deeper understanding of each other. When holding a celebration, it is important that we do so with the support and encouragement of our children. When families gather, these may be times of stress, so planning ahead may make things run more smoothly. Given the structure of many families today, grandchildren may have many places to visit on holidays based on step grandparents and a large extended family so it is best to take your lead from your children in order to help alleviate any tension that may arise.

"My paternal grandmother lived to be 92 and had 32 grandchildren. She taught me religion, right from wrong and how to eat organically healthy. My special day with her was always my birthday. I would have lunch with her, just her and I. It was a very special event every year in my life." MONIQUE, GRANDDAUGHTER

1. CELEBRATE YOU: Grandparent's Day: 2016 – Sept 11th, 2017 Sept 10th! Have fun!

2. RITUALS: Special occasions can be the beginning of new and wonderful traditions that happen every year on these memorable events. Plan with your children and grandchildren how you want to celebrate.

3. CANDY: Candy can become a real trigger in some families when parents are not pleased when grandparents ply their grandchildren with sweets. So a reasonable balance must be maintained and parents' wishes should prevail.

"When I rushed home from school for lunch, I knew when my grandmother was visiting because I would spy salmon sandwiches cut into triangles on our kitchen table and I knew she was hiding somewhere in the house. The front closest was her favourite spot and when I would find her there, she always had a package of Life Savers for me to take back to school. I was a great hit with my friends. Always one of my favourite memories!" LYNN, GRANDDAUGHTER

4. TREATS: Create treasures for party goers by placing small objects inside a paper tube. Wrap in fancy paper longer than the tube and twist the ends. Tie with a ribbon or string. Place each of these on the plates of the party guests.

5. FAMILY BIRTHDAY: Family birthdays are important events. Help your grandchildren prepare a special craft or card for their loved ones. Plan a new game, pin the eye patch on the pirate, smack a Pinata, decorate cupcakes in your favourite flavours etc.

6. FOOD: Food is so often tied to wonderful memories during seasonal or family celebrations. Whether it is making latkes, eating chicken wings, Empanadas, Torteire, beaver tails or plantain, food is a great way to celebrate!

 FURTHER READING:

Festival Foods: World Of Recipes by McCulloch
Festival Foods by Vaughan

Kids Around The World Celebrate by Jones
Festivals Family & Food by Carey & Large

7. TEA PARTY: Plan a tea party with your finest china tea cups and interesting tea pots. Serve party sandwiches and dress up in fancy hats and gloves. You may want to make your own party hats with paper plates, ribbons, artificial flowers and other goodies from your craft supplies. What else are you saving your good china for?

"In a childhood world where I was treated as an inferior to the many adults in my life, my grandparents, with whom I spent a lot of time, treated me not exactly as an equal but as fully formed person with ideas and desires that mattered as much as theirs. One of my fondest memories is sitting with both of them in their front room with our cups of instant coffee watching the news and reviewing the race results in the newspaper." CHARLIE, PARENT

8. SPECIAL PLATE: Go shopping to a store that sells place settings or perhaps an antique or thrift shop and have your child pick out their favourite plate. This plate will be used for all special occasions at your house and it is just for them. Let all your grandchildren chose their own special plate.

9. WRAPPING PAPER: Make wrapping paper by blowing paint across the paper with a straw or fold the paper for an ink blot design. Let dry.

10. BIKE PARADE: When the weather co-operates and it might be the first time you can get your bikes out of the basement, decorate your bikes and go for a ride!

11. TEDDY BEAR PICNIC: Have a teddy bear picnic and read the story about *Goldilocks and the Three Bears* or *Winnie The Pooh*. You might serve honey tea or peanut butter and honey sandwiches or Teddy Grahams. Sing the song: *The Teddy Bear's Picnic.*

12. BACKWARDS PARTY: Try something different and do everything backwards. Wear your shirt and hat backwards, eat that birthday cake before the main meal.

"Sharing holidays and special events with your grandchildren sets the stage for their memories of you." PAM, NANA

Celebrate the special events that are special for your family. Here are just a few suggestions:

Hallowe'en

1. HALLOWEEN WREATH: Shape a coat hanger into a circle and begin by tying strips of green garbage bags until you have gone all around the hanger. Spray it orange and you have a Halloween wreath!

2. PUMPKINS: Create pumpkin faces on painted paper plates or orange construction paper and tape them to the window.

3. TABLE DECORATIONS: Decorate a plastic tablecloth with Halloween stickers.

4. GHOSTS: Cut a thin sponge into a ghost shape. You can dip the sponges into white paint and create a scary ghost picture. You can also use a piece of black or orange construction paper. The same can be done with a pumpkin or cat shape.

5. BATS: Read the book *Stellaluna* by Janell Cannon then create a bat by cutting out two black circles, cut one in half with a jagged cut and these two pieces become the wings. Create a face, punch a hole in the top and hang from the ceiling.

"One of my fondest memories is our involvement in my granddaughter's first Hallowe'en. She was almost a year old and my daughter had dressed her up as a pumpkin.

She had no idea what was going on but we adults had the time of our lives! I have about a hundred pictures I could show you!! Priceless!" EMMA, GRANNY BENNETT

Valentine's Day

1. VALENTINE HEARTS: You may have some eager sowers in your family. They begin by cutting out two heart shapes out of red material, felt etc. and using a Bodkin needle, sew around the edges leaving a little hole in which to stuff in stuffing! Sew closed. Presto a heart to give away.

2. SPONGE PAINTING: Cut sponges into heart shapes and dab away.

3. GET FANCY: Help your grandchild make their own homemade Valentines for their friends with all your craft supplies. Don't leave anyone out.

4. CAKES: You can create cakes for just about any celebration by cutting them into appropriate shapes and decorating them with coloured icing and sprinkles of all kinds.

Easter

1. OUTSTANDING EGGS: Colour eggs with food colouring, boiling water and vinegar.

2. THE HUNT IS ON: This can become a yearly ritual by creating word clues or picture clues for younger children. Take pictures of various parts of your house or apartment. You hand your grandchild the first picture (ie: the laundry basket in front of the dryer). When they get to the basket there is another picture there and so it goes. They follow the picture clues until they find their Easter eggs. The older the children, the more complex the search and don't forget to send them outside!

Winter Holidays

1. SNOWFLAKES: If your grandchild has good scissor skills, this is a fun activity. Start with a square, fold it in half diagonally to make a triangle. Fold the triangle in half and again. Cut out designs along the three sides of the triangle. Unfold and hang or put them on your window.

2. FOOD: There are so many wonderful memories that revolve around food for special occasions. Create your own memories with your grandchild – try to create a variety of frozen healthy treats!

3. CENTERPIECE: You can create a simple centrepiece after an outdoor walk where you gather items that can be pushed into florist oasis. Add a candle and ribbons then place on an interesting plate or saucer.

4. CHAINS: Making chains is a simple experience for decorating the house for the holidays. Cut out strips of paper about 1-2 inches wide in the colours you have chosen. With a dab of glue or a swish of a glue stick on the end of one of the strips, fold over and you have the first chain. Insert the next strip of paper into the circle and glue away.

5. FESTIVAL OF LIGHTS: Almost every group celebrates a festival of lights during this time of the year. You can make candles together (see the David Suzuki website).

6. ORNAMENTS: Clear balls are available and you can put treasures inside and paint the outside as well. You might do this every year and include pictures of your grandchild and see how they grow over the years. It will be fun to unpack this ornament for the house.

"Being a grandparent is a gift. To be able to share in your child's children is a privilege." PAM, NANA

LET'S GO
OUTSIDE

MY NANA AND PAPA, CARTER, AGE 8

OUT AND ABOUT

"Grandchildren are the best present your children can give you.
Our grandchildren bring new life to any situation. Remember
when your children were little and they noticed small things -
a butterfly flitting through the garden, an ant crawling across
the path? Well, grandchildren bring that back - a sense of
wonder in a world we too often overlook or forget. Sharing
the pleasure in simple things and moments is a gift from them
to us." PAMELA, NANA

With rising issues about childhood obesity and lack of activity, grandparents have an opportunity to model active engagement in the out of doors. Environmentalist and author Rachel Carson states that *"if a child is to keep alive his inborn sense of wonder, he needs the companionship of at least one adult who can share it, rediscovering with him the joy, excitement, and mystery of the world we live in."* We know that children will protect what they know. A more recent book that has become a must read is Richard Louv's book: *Last Child In The Woods: Saving Our Children From Nature-Deficit Disorder.* His work presents evidence that exposure to nature is essential for a child's healthy physical and emotional development. His work has helped to create an international back-to-nature campaign.

The outdoor environment has the potential to provide a rich array of flexible materials for children's play. In fact, in many cases, nature's open ended natural materials are literally right outside our doors. Children love to interact with variables. Natural materials such as rocks, leaves, twigs, sand, and water will all add depth to the children's play and there is no better place to do this than in the out of doors!

Simple Ideas

1. TUMMY TIME AND GRASS: Take the time with your grandchild to really see the common things in our environment that we sometimes take for granted. Watch your new grandchild putting their feet on the grass for the first time, how do they react? Encourage tummy time to really feel the grass, smell it, lay your cheek on it – explore!

2. WIND CHIMES: Wind chimes can be made with just about anything that makes a noise. Hang it outdoors on a tree branch and place the baby on a blanket underneath.

3. ROCK DISCOVERIES: Young children often find rocks fascinating and collecting them provides great opportunities to talk about their size, shape, colour, hard, smooth, rocks with speckles, rocks with stripes etc.

4. ROLL OVER: Moving old logs unearths critters that hide there and it is always a surprise.

5. RAKING: When fall comes raking up the leaves will provide lots of fun!

6. LEAF GATHERING: Encourage your grandchild to collect leaves just for the fun of collecting. Toddlers love to collect and dump! Nothing is more fun than jumping into a great pile of leaves. Make leaf angels instead of snow angels in the leaves. You might also create a maze with the leaves and create a fun chasing game.

7. LEAF CATCHING: On a really windy day when lots of leaves are falling, make leaf catchers out of lightweight recyclable plastic bags and try to catch the leaves before they hit the ground!

8. SOCKS FOR YOUR SHOES: Pull on some oversized socks over everyone's shoes and go for a walk. An interesting forest, a park or a field would be great! Take off your socks and check them out with a magnifying glass. What has hitched a ride on your socks? Put your socks into a plastic bag and give them a little water. Put the bag in the sun and watch what happens! Try planting your sock – what happens?

9. SHOELACE WALK: Take along a shoelace on a nature walk. How many objects can be strung on a shoelace?

10. STICKY WALK: Form a piece of cardboard into a circle to create a bracelet. Place a strip of double-sided tape, sticky side up around the circle. Take your grandchild on a nature walk and find out what they have collected on their bracelet when you get home.

11. WEEDING: Helping to weed the garden will be much appreciated. It is also an opportunity to help children learn the difference between a weed and a flower!

12. DRIVEWAYS: Gravel driveways are just the thing for creating road ways for little cars and trucks.

13. SAND PLAY: You can purchase a plastic sand box with a lid to keep out the critters and you will find that the children, with added loose props, can spend a very long time pouring and shoveling.

14. SAND TENT: One way to protect your sand and shelter your grandchild from the sun is to set up a pup tent and pour in the sand and some sand toys! Zip it up at night to keep out the critters.

15. SAND MOLDS: Sand and water together make great opportunities for mold making. Provide a variety of interesting containers for creating – cups, bowls, boxes, incorporate containers from a wide range of cultures, and interesting scoops, spoons, ladles and access to a hose.

 FURTHER READING:

Sift And Shout by Granovetter & James
Dirt: Jump Into Science by Tomecek
A Handful Of Dirt by Bial

More complex Ideas

1. DIRT FRIENDS: Children love dirt! Mix it with water and watch the play expand. Dig up a couple of capfuls of dirt. Dump them onto a piece of white paper and using a magnifying glass examine the dirt to see what insects, plants or rocks they can find. Then use a small sifter to sift dirt through and really get a good look at all the little creatures. The soil is loaded with microorganisms, it's alive!

 FURTHER READING:

Jump Into Science: Dirt by Tomecek & Woodman
A Handful Of Dirt by Bial
Dirt: The Scoop On Soil by Rosinsky
The Dirt On Dirt by Bourgeois
The Amazing Dirt Book by Bourgeois

2. BE A DETECTIVE: Where does your plant live – in the sun or the shade? Really examine plants by tracing, drawing or making a rubbing of the leaf. What shape is it? What colour is it? Are both sides of the leaf the same? Are all the leaves on the plant the same? What does the edge of the leaf look and feel like? Are there flowers on the plant? How many petals does it have? What colour is it? What's in the centre of the flower? Does it smell? What shape is the stem? Squeeze it, what happens? What does the root system look like? Can you find any insects? So many questions!

3. TREE STUMPS: Older children may be intrigued by discovering the age of a tree. You may want to guess how old you and your grandchild think the tree is before you start counting. Look at the rings that were formed. How close and how wide apart the rings are indicate the weather conditions at that time in the tree's life. The rings are widest at the beginning when the tree was first growing and very close together in a season that was very dry.

4. PLANT A SPECIAL TREE: Plant a special tree for each of your grandchildren, perhaps to commemorate a special event! There are so many spectacular trees especially those that bloom in the spring as new growth "explodes". Trees such as Forsythia, Lilacs and Magnolia trees are spectacular examples. A dwarf tree is just right for young children. They take up very little space, some trees will bear fruit within a year or two of planting and the fruit will be easy for your grandchildren to reach. Others will provide interesting colour like a Japanese Maple. This memory tree will be one your grandchild can return to as they grow older. A fun project would be to photograph your grandchild standing next to the tree over many years – a wonderful keepsake.

 FURTHER READING:

My Favourite Tree: Terrific Trees of North America by Iverson
The Giving Tree by Silverstein
Old Elm Speaks by O'Connell George

5. WISHING TREE: Having children record their wishes on a *Wish Tree* provides an opportunity to talk about how we may make the world a better place. They can record their wishes on a piece of tag board with a hole punched in the top and laminated. Wishes can be hung with string or ribbon and hung from the tree.

6.   NATURE WALKS: Take six quart baskets, sturdy brown bags, sand pails or a Ziploc bag and collect items during your walk. This is a great opportunity to expand vocabulary and an opportunity to encourage sorting and classifying of items based on their own observations of the collection − big and small, pretty, ugly, smooth edges, jagged edges, ones I want to take home etc.

7.   HIKES: As your grandchildren grow and are more able, go for hikes and explore national parks. A great way for you both to keep active!

8.   KITES: Fly a Kite or a paper airplane.

 FURTHER READING:

> *Curious George Flies A Kite by Rey*
> *Kites Sail High by Heller*
> *Let's Fly A Kite by Murphy*
> *The Great Kite Book by Schmidt*
> *Kite Flying by Lin*

9.   BIKES: With helmets on, look for bike pathways in your community and go for rides together. Stop for a picnic along the way!

10. CAR WASH: Lots of soap and lots of water make for great fun when you wash the car together. You can wash bikes while you are at it or dolls or...

11. CAR REPAIR: Teach your grandchild how to check the oil, water and wiper fluid in a car.

12. TIME FOR DOING NOTHING: We never find enough time for simple things − spread out a blanket and have your grandchildren lie on their backs and watch the sky − look for cloud shapes. Over time, help the children identify the different types of clouds. Some of the easiest to identify are Cirrus, the highest clouds made of ice crystals, Stratus clouds which are low hanging and stretch across the sky and Cumulus clouds, the fluffy ones and the ones we most often see on clear days!

FURTHER READING:

The Cloud Book by dePaola
Clouds by Rockwell & Lessac
Little Cloud by Carle

13. PUMPKINS! Creating a pumpkin patch is great fun where space allows. Your grandchildren can estimate and weigh a variety of pumpkins, guess how many seeds, pick out their favourite to take home etc.

FURTHER READING:

Big Pumpkin by Silverman
The Pumpkin Patch Parable by Curtis Higgs
Pumpkin Soup Book & CD by Cooper
The Pumpkin Runner by Arnold
Seed, Sprout, Pumpkin Pie by Esbaum
Too Many Pumpkins & CD by White

14. MY PERSONAL PUMPKIN: When the pumpkin is young and green and using a large nail, write the child's name into the rind. Don't go too deep. Point the name to the sun and watch what happens over time.

15. CARING FOR OTHERS: Perhaps there are others in your community that you can help – those that need their leaves raked or driveways shovelled. This is a good project for you and your grandchild to do together.

"Throughout her life, my Grandma took on the role of care-giver. She would always go out of her way to make sure everyone around her was happy and felt taken care of. Near the end of her battle with cancer it was my turn to make sure she felt taken care of. She was quite weak but still loved getting outside to see the wildlife that surrounded her

property and take in some sun. We'd walk up and down the driveway - at a snail's pace - not saying much, just appreciating our time together arm in arm." ALEXANDRA, GRANDDAUGHTER

 ## CRITTERS IN THE OUT OF DOORS

Simple Ideas

1. BIRD BATH MADE EASY: Take a plastic flower pot and turn it upside down. Take a plastic bowl or a planting tray big enough to cover the top of the pot and glue. Presto, an inexpensive bird bath!

2. BIRD FEATHERS: It is not unusual to find bird feathers. See if your grandchildren can match the feathers to the bird. Look at feathers carefully and gently pull apart the web of the feather. Look for tiny barbules that project from the barbs. Use magnifying glasses to help. Feathers also insulate and waterproof a bird's body. Find out more!

3. NESTING BALL: Collect a variety of bits and pieces such as yarn, ribbon, string, lint from the clothes dryer, anything a bird could use to create a nest. Place all the items in a mesh onion bag and hang where your grandchildren can see it and birds will have access. If you use very colourful items you may see them reappear in a bird's nest nearby.

4. BIRD FOOD TREE: Hang popcorn, cranberries, dried fruits, or pretzels from tree branches to create your own unique food tree.

5. QUICK AND EASY FOOD: In winter, (not in summer, the peanut butter can spoil and make the birds sick) roll a pine cone or a paper toilet roll in peanut butter and then roll in bird seed and hang outside. Be careful putting out bread for birds. If it goes moldy, it can make the birds sick.

More complex Ideas

1. CARING FOR BIRDS: Set up feeding trays that can be kept stocked with seeds all year round in your backyard or on your balcony. Perhaps you can build a bird feeder together? Who comes to the feeder? Robert Bateman's book on *Backyard Birds* is spectacular! Keep watch since this will also be an opportunity to see how often squirrels "steal" the bird's food not to mention night time visitors like racoons!

2. BIRDS IN WINTER: Fill pie plates with water and add bird seed, place a small cup at the top of the pie plate then freeze. Dip the pie plate momentarily in hot water and your frozen creation will come free of the pan. Remove the cup and you will have a hole through which to hang your feeder. This can also be done using a Bundt pan so you will have a large hole in the middle.

 FURTHER READING:

Backyard Birds Of Winter by Lerner
Birds In Winter by Duquet
Feeding Winter Birds by Waldon

3. GOURD NESTS: When gourds or pumpkins are harvested, some can be kept to create bird nests by cutting them in half and filling with bird seed or carving out windows and doors and placing bird seed inside. Hang these creations in a spot where your grandchildren can see what happens.

4. BIRD SOUNDS: Find a local birding book and pick two or three of the most common birds in your area. Your local library should be able to help and they may have a CD with bird sounds. Help your grandchild find the birds using binoculars when possible and try and match the bird with their song.

 FURTHER READING:

Bird Calls by Gallo
Twenty Five Bird Songs For Children by Olds
Birdscapes: A Pop Up Celebration Of Bird Songs In Stereo Sound by Chu

The Songs Of Birds: Stories And Poems From Many Cultures by Lupton

5. HUMMINGBIRDS: You can attract Hummingbirds by dissolving one part sugar to three parts hot water. Add beet juice since the birds are attracted to the colour red. Pour into a clear plastic bird feeder designed for Hummingbirds and hang from a tree branch.

 FURTHER READING:

> *Birds, Nests And Eggs by Boring*
> *Backyard Birds by Stray Nolting, Latimer, Peterson*
> *Birds. National Audubon Society First Field Guides by Weidensaul*
> *How Do Birds Find Their Way by Gans*
> *Bird by Burnie*
> *Letter Birds ABC Bird Book by Spremulli*

"My Grandfather and I built a bird house together. We bought a kit from the hardware store and after a great deal of effort and lots of glue, we had a bird house. I remember we painted it bright red and I spent hours with binoculars waiting for the birds to arrive. My Grandfather provided the names for all the birds. He was amazing!" GRIFFITH, GRANDSON

6. ANIMALS: There are lots of interesting books about critters you may find at home or on your walks.

 FURTHER READING:

> *Animals At Home by Lock*
> *Pop Up Animal Homes. National Geographic Action Book by Terreson*
> *Animal Homes by Chessen & Chanko*

Animal Homes by Squire
Animal Homes. Usborne Lift The Flap Book by Martin

7. ANTS, ANTS AND MORE ANTS: One of the easiest critters to study outdoors is ants because they are so plentiful. Use magnifying glasses to study ants and
the ways that they move. Ants use their antennae to smell with. Watch them go!
Having trouble finding them - leave a variety of tiny bits of foods that the children
think ants might like out overnight. What happens in the morning? Were other
insects attracted to the food?

8. TERRARIUM/ANT PALACE: Make a terrarium or an ant's palace from a
variety of materials – plastic bottles, sand, plants, interesting rocks etc.

 FURTHER READING:

Adventures Among Ants: A Global Safari
With A Cast of Trillions by Moffett
National Geographic Readers: Ants by Steward
Life And Times Of The Ant by Micucci

9. LADYBUGS: Ladybugs are wonderful additions to any garden because they love to
eat pests that can be harmful to plants. You can buy Ladybugs from many nurseries.
Be gentle with them, they are tiny!

 FURTHER READING:

Big Book of Bugs by Greenaway
I Like Bugs by Wise Brown
Bugs, Bugs, Bugs, by Dussling

10. SPIDER FOG WALK: Nothing is more impressive than finding spider webs on a
foggy day. The moisture in the fog is transferred to spider webs making them very
noticeable and when the sun shines through them – amazing!

11. SPIDERS ARE ARACHNIDS: With a quick check on the internet, you can become an insect specialist. Spiders are Arachnids and have 4 pairs of legs and two body segments. Though many species have multiple eyes, most spiders do not see well. They use sensory feelers directly in front of their mouths to feel and handle their prey. All spiders use silk and spin it from spinnerets at the rear of their abdomen.

 FURTHER READING:

Insects: Eyewitness Books by Mound
Spinning Spiders by Berman
Tarantula Spiders by Murray
Child's Guide To Insects And Spiders by Johnson
The Itsy Bitsy Spider by Trapani

"I so remember my grandparent's garden. It was the most beautiful garden I had ever seen. They always encouraged me to help them weed and care for the plants. Whenever I smell lilacs to this day, I remember how my grandmother would always send me home with my arms full." JASMINE, GRANDDAUGHTER

 PLANTING FUN!

If space allows a garden is a great opportunity to share your own stories about gardening in the past and planting some of your favourites. If you don't have garden space, planting in containers can accomplish the same thing! Perhaps each spring you and your grandchildren could plant a different type of garden. The following are some ideas for that special project.

Simple Ideas

1. INTERESTING CONTAINERS: Plants can be planted in a variety of different containers – have your grandchildren look for unusual containers and plant away – old boots, sneakers, tea cups, baskets, watering cans, pots, coconut shells, hats etc. A great way to encourage recycling is to have children plant in food cans (drill some holes in the bottom) or cereal boxes with waxed paper interiors.

2. PERSONALIZED CONTAINERS: Your grandchildren can take clay pots and decorate these by gluing twine or yarn around the edges or paint the pot with acrylic paint.

3. MARKING PLANTINGS: Using wooden paint stir sticks, your grandchildren can decorate their marker so they will be able to identify their individual plants.

4. DREAM GARDEN: A good idea, when thinking about spring and it's still cold and icy outside, is to create a dream garden. Use old gardening magazines, seed books etc. and have your grandchildren cut out and make their own dream gardens.

5. PLANT FAST GROWERS: Plant flowers and vegetables that are fast growers or are impressive when grown – corn, sunflowers, radishes, pumpkins. Track on a calendar the planting date and the growth of the plants.

6. SPROUTS: Sprouts are seeds that have just begun to germinate so they grow very quickly. There are lots of varieties, snow pea seeds, alfalfa, chickpea, mung beans, lentils, azuki beans, watercress etc.

7. WHICH SEEDS DO I PICK?: Larger seeds will make it easier for little hands to plant so try radishes, peas, beets, and spinach. Tulips, onions, garlic and potatoes are also fun to plant.

8. BULBS: For a great spring showing, plants bulbs in the fall.

9. POPCORN GARDEN: If you love popcorn, fill a pie plate with potting soil and plant the kernels.

10. FLOWER PHOTOS: A fun game may be to take photos of flowers and herbs in your garden and then see if your grandchildren can match the picture with the real flower. You can also print off two of each picture and have your grandchildren play a matching game or a concentration game. For a longer explore you might take pictures in your community and take a walk to find the match.

11. PANSIES: Pansies are unique flowers since they often look like they have faces and often one of the first plants to be successfully planted in the spring. Press them between pages of a book and use them when dried for art projects, fancy note paper etc.

12. DANDELIONS: If dandelions are popping up everywhere, it must be spring! Many people spend a lot of time weeding them out of their lawns but they are in fact very useful. Try making some dandelion tea! They also make great bouquets for the table and if they aren't picked, a fluffy round seed head forms. Watch the seeds

float to the ground like little parachutes. An old tale says that after one blow, the number of seeds left is the time of day or the number of children you will have! Other people believe that your wish will come true if you blow on the seeds.

13. CARROT TOPS: Take the carrots grown in the garden, eat all the way up to the greens leaving the curly tops. Plant the tops and wait and watch. Beet, Turnip and Pineapple tops can also be used.

 FURTHER READING:

The Carrot Seed by Kraus
Curious George The Perfect Carrot by Rey
Carrots Grow Underground by Schuh
Just Enough Carrots by Murphy
Going For Carrots by Cook
The Giant Carrot by Peck

14. BEAN SEED IN A JAR: Fill a glass jar with wet paper towels and place lima beans (great because they are so big) right up against the side of the jar. Place the jar in a sunny spot and see what happens.

15. JACK AND THE BEANSTALK: Recreate this story with the children and collect a variety of beans, green ones, purple ones, red ones and plant them. What happens?

 FURTHER READING:

Jack And The Beanstalk by Ottolenghi
Jack And The Beanstalk by Kellogg
Jack And The Beanstalk by Cech
Jump At The Sun: Jack And The Beanstalk by Kurt

16. MR. EGGHEAD: Cut the top off an egg shell and fill the shell with soil. Sprinkle with grass seed and make a face on the shell. Put the egg into an eggcup and place your Eggheads in the sun and watch what happens. Does your Mr. Egghead need a haircut? How long did it take?

17. MR. POTATO HEAD: Scrub a potato and cut off the top. Your grandchildren can make a face with bits of carrots, green peppers, mushrooms etc. Where the white of the potato is exposed, sprinkle with grass seed or sprouts and in 2-3 days the potato will have "hair".

More complex Ideas

1. COMMUNITY GARDENS: Is there a community garden where people come together to plant in an area in your neighbourhood? Your grandchildren could have a section of the garden to plant. Perhaps there is a plot of land that is not well cared for, could your grandchildren "take over" the space and improve its appearance with their planting efforts?

2. FUNNY NAME GARDEN: Your grandchildren will enjoy creating a Funny Name Garden by planting only plants with unusual or funny names – Bleeding Hearts, Japanese Blood Grass, Snake Weed, Spider Wort, Lamb's Ear, Elephant Ears, Joe Pye Weed, Cattails, Cat Nip, Jenny Green Teeth, just to name a few!

3. WEIRD GARDEN: There are unusual fruits and vegetables that will provide great opportunities for you and your grandchild to compare and contrast if planted beside the "ordinary" types – red brussel sprouts, sweet corn "Indian Summer" (white, red, purple and yellow), golden raspberries etc. Your may want to check with your local nurseries for other ideas that will work in your zone.

4. MYSTERY GARDEN: Take a variety of seeds and stir them all together. Plant and wait for the results. You may want to take photos as they grow.

5. PLANT A HUGE GARDEN: Let your grandchildren decide what to plant and where – they will learn by trial and error. Have your grandchildren pick out seeds or plants that will grow to be giants – pumpkins, long carrots, muskmelons, jumbo cabbage, cucumber, giant flowers etc.

6. PLANT A LITTLE GARDEN: There are many types of small seedling trays that allow for the start-up of seeds when your space is limited. When cost allows, the experience becomes more personal if each grandchild has their own tray. Another idea is to use an egg carton after giving it a wash, fill the egg holes with soil and plant seeds in each hole. Some quick to grow seeds are marigold, candytuft,

cornflower, nasturtium (leaves and seedpods can be eaten), poppies, and mallow. Most of these germinate in 1-3 weeks. This is a great activity if you want to get a jump start on your spring planting!

7.   PLANT A FAIRY GARDEN: There are several wonderful books about Fairies. Read these stories to your grandchildren and then plan and plant a fairy garden. You may also want to read *Fairy Houses Everywhere!* By Tracy and Barry Kane and also add some homes for your fairies. Draw a big circle and create a trench around the outside of your fairy garden. Plant large grasses in the trench or even sunflowers. They will grow and provide a private space for your grandchildren. Don't forget to leave a doorway. Plant away in the middle and include items such as leaves, wood chips, rocks, pine cones, sticks, little bells or chimes and anything that is safe that could be used for fairy dust! It's also a good time to talk about fairies they may know – Tinkerbell, The Sugar Plum Fairy, The Fairy Godmother!

 FURTHER READING:

Flower Fairies Of The Garden by Barker
My Garden Of Fairy Flowers by Barker
How To Find Flower Fairies by Barker
The Secret Fairy Garden by Zobel-Nolan

8.   ZEN GARDENS: Perhaps each grandchild could have their own Zen Garden if materials and funds allow. A great opportunity to discuss gardens from a wide range of cultures and the influences that make them special.

9.   BONSAI GARDEN: Bonsai gardens are a Japanese art form using miniature trees grown in containers. Give it a try!

10.   A CACTUS GARDEN: For those without a green thumb, you might provide your grandchildren with a variety of succulents that survive in areas with little water. A great opportunity to talk about deserts. Have your grandchildren feel the plants carefully? How are they different from other plants they might have seen?

11.   PIZZA GARDEN: Choose herbs and plants that will be a welcome addition to a homemade pizza. You might even plant in a circle just like a pizza. Divide each section and add plum tomatoes, peppers, onions, parsley, oregano, garlic, sweet basil etc.

12. SALSA GARDEN: Add onions, garlic bulbs, tomato seedlings, chilli pepper seedlings, green pepper, coriander seedlings and don't forget to include marigolds to keep the bugs away. Harvest, chop and eat!

13. GARDEN SALAD BASKET: Find a very large wicker basket or interesting container and line it with plastic. Poke in some holes. Add soil and compost and plant a variety of lettuce seeds or seedlings. Plant oak leaf lettuce, Boston lettuce, ruby red, spinach, arugula, mustard, radishes, beets, cucumber, cherry tomatoes, scallions, and spinach

14. ALPHABET GARDEN: If you have lots of room, this might be a fun project. Begin by finding a flower or vegetable for every letter of the alphabet and plant it – i.e.: A is for aster, B is for balloon flower – Z is for zinnia! The Hayes Valley Farm, an urban farming project in San Francisco has posted many photos of their Alphabet Garden and list plants for planting from A-Z!

@ www.flickr.com/photos/edibleoffice/sets/72157624454856630/

15. SUNFLOWER GARDEN: Organize a picnic lunch to be eaten under giant sunflowers. Encourage your grandchildren to imagine what it would be like to be a little person. Think Gulliver's Travels!

16. TEA GARDEN: Plant peppermint, lavender, lemon verbena, rose hips, bergamont, marjoram, chamomile, jasmine for example. You can purchase small gauze tea bags and make your own special teas.

17. PETER RABBIT GARDEN: Reading Beatrix Potter's books may inspire your grandchildren to plant a garden that they think Peter Rabbit would love to visit.

18. SMELLY GARDEN: Plant fragrant roses, lavender, lemon thyme, sage, lemon balm, geraniums, sweet alyssum, lemon verbena, peonies, phlox, lilies, marigolds or sweet woodruff.

19. NAME GARDEN: Find plants that might have the names of your grandchildren and plant them in a special name garden – jack-in-the pulpit, johnny jump up, sweet william, rowan, basil, sage, heather, hyacinth, iris, lily, rose, violet etc.

20. BUTTERFLY GARDENS: Butterflies love to visit certain plants looking for sweet nectar and they are attracted to flowers by strong colours and a sweet scent.

Some favourites are butterfly bush, marigolds, zinnias, asters, borage, nasturtium, milkweed, sedum, cosmos, black-eyed susan, bee balm, phlox, snapdragons etc. and plant them in a sunny spot. Binoculars will help you get a close up look.

FURTHER READING:

Butterfly Butterfly: A Book Of Colours by Horacek
From Caterpillar To Butterfly Big Book by Heiligman
The Buterfly Alphabet Book by Cassie
Caterpillars, Bugs And Butterflies by Boring
I Spy A Butterfly by Marzollo

21. PLANT AN HERB GARDEN: There are so many fragrant and interesting herbs to plant. A visit to a local nursery will help you decide which ones to plant. Infants and toddlers will love herbs such as mint, basil, dill, oregano and they are safe to explore.

22. HERB IDENTIFICATION: As your grandchildren become more familiar with the herbs from their garden, play a guessing game with them. Blindfold your grandchildren and ask if they can identify the herb just by smell and touch? You may want to show older children how medicines are made from flowers and herbs such as alfalfa, horsetail, plantain, red clover, yarrow etc.

FURTHER READING:

Kids Herb Book by Tierra
Herb The Vegetarian Dragon by Bass
The Yummy Alphabet Book: Herbs, Spices And
Other Natural Flavors by Pallotta
Ancient Medical Technology: From Herbs to Scalpels

23. CORN HUSK DOLLS: Dry corn husks in a cool dark space and when you are ready to make the dolls, soak the husks in warm water for a short period of time. Let your grandchildren experiment with raffia to create a head and body. You might provide accessories for the doll such as wool, crepe paper, googly eyes, ribbon or

other items from your craft supplies. To provide more colourful versions, try dying the husks by adding food colouring as they are soaking in warm water.

24. SCARECROW: Create an interesting scarecrow to protect your garden by stuffing old clothes. A pillow case or pantyhose makes a good head. You might make an edible scarecrow by adding plants in pockets for the birds.

25. SEED BALLS: Use 3 cups of clay, 2 cups of compost and ½ cup of seeds and mix together. Start with the dry ingredients first and then slowly add water until the soil is moist but not sticky. Roll into balls that are about 1 inch in diameter. Toss the balls into the garden, keep an eye on them and make sure to water them. Record which seeds grow from the balls. See more information at:

@ www.evergreen.ca

 FURTHER READING:

Green Thumbs: A Kids Activity Guide To Indoor
And Outdoor Activities by Carlson
Organic Guide For Kids by School
Kids First Gardening Book by Hendy
How Does Your Garden Grow? By Matthews
Gardening Activities For 3-5 Year Olds by Quin
Jumbo Book Of Gardening by Morris
Roots, Shoots, Buckets And Boots: Gardening
Together With Children by Lovejoy
Kids In The Garden by McCorquodale

"My grandmother was amazing! She would come to our school and pick my sister and me for lunch once a week. We called it "Granny Day". We would go to the park and play until it was time to go back to school and we always returned with a sack of candies. You have no idea how popular we were at recess." ALEX, GRANDSON

MY NONNY, ERIC, AGE 3

FUN WITH WATER

Water play fascinates children, it moves, it can be manipulated, it drips, it makes noises, it can be dammed up, can be channelled along the ground, it is essential for life and much more.

Simple Ideas

1. WATER PLAY: Pour it, wash dollies with it, use it in squirt bottles to "paint" the fence, make puddles and splash. Water play can also be a soothing and calming activity for your grandchild when challenges arise.

2. WATER GARDEN: Create your own water garden in an old aquarium or water-proof container and plant water plants. A large pot can be used that includes a small pump to create a water feature. Your water feature is sure to lure frogs and toads to come and play!

3. WATER WALK: If you are lucky enough to live near the water, collect rocks worn smooth by water, look for drift wood, shells, beach glass, and interesting rocks and paint them. Take along a picnic and have a great water day.

 FURTHER READING:

Curious George Goes To The Beach by Rey

Beach Day by Roosa
At The Beach by Rockwell
Beach Babies Wear Shades by Sinclair Colman
Where Is Baby's Beach Ball? by Katz

"I am not sure what my granddaughter will remember of these first few years, but I always will. These early years are such a gift to grandparents. I hope she remembers a few of the times we played, the beach and our hugs. Her energy, her laugh and her big hugs just make me feel young again! Let's hope there are more coming!" RICK, PAPA

4. SHELLS: There are so many wonderful shells. Become a collector!

 FURTHER READING:

Seashells By The Seashore by Berkes & Noreika
There Was An Old Lady Who Swallowed A Shell by Colandro
Eyewitness: Shells by Arthur
Shells by Franco-Feeney & Sorra

5. THE SPRINKLER: Get out the sprinkler and let the fun begin!

6. SLIP SLIDING AWAY: A sheet of plastic, a slight incline and some running water is all you need for this type of water play!

7. SWIMMING POOL: Fill a little plastic pool with water and when interest begins to lag, add play materials that float and sink or try adding safe liquid soap and watch the fun!

8. BUBBLE FUN: Chasing bubbles is always an enjoyable event no matter what the child's age. Straws in the bubble mixture will give your young grandchild an

opportunity to understand that pushing air through the straw produces bubbles (add Glycerine for stronger bubbles). An alternative is to cut the bottom off a single water bottle and the children then dip the open end into the solution and blow! Big bubbles!! They can also see the different colours as the light shines through the bubbles. Give this a try in winter, what happens to the bubbles?

 FURTHER READING:

Benny's Big Bubble by O'Connor
Bubble Trouble by Mahy
Pop! A Book About Bubbles by Brubaker Breadley
Bubble Bubble by Mayer

9. BUBBLE WRAP: Keep bubble wrap that often comes inside parcels sent through the mail. Even older children will have fun stomping on the bubble wrap!

10. SQUIRT BOTTLES: Nothing is more fun that using squirt bottles on plants, walls, equipment and most of all on each other!

11. RUNNING WATER: Can you create a path for the water from your tap, angling the water with stones and pebbles toward the sand area? Use tubes, plumbing pipes, clear hose pieces, bamboo and wood to help your grandchildren create water pathways.

12. WASHING OUR CLOTHES: A great way to help children learn about evaporation is to have them collect clothes and encourage them to wash them. Adding soap changes the whole experience and rinsing is great fun. Your grandchildren can hang the clothes on a clothes line outside or hang on a fence and have them monitor the drying process.

13. CAR WASH: A great opportunity to engage your grandchildren in caring for their bikes as well as watching what happens when soap and water are mixed. Be prepared - lots of other things often get washed in the process.

14. PUDDLE FUN: Don't forget to look at the surface of the puddle. Can you see your face? Touch the puddle, what happens? Can you float things in the puddles? Draw a chalk line around the edge of the puddle and watch what happens when the sun comes up.

15. MUD, MUD AND MORE MUD: There is nothing that provides a more complex sensory experience than exploring mud. Mud is squishy and it is great to investigate. Squish it, push it, splash it. Keep the hose handy!

FURTHER READING:

Mud Pies And Other Recipes. A Cookbook For Dolls by Winslow
Mud Pies And Other Recipes by Wilson
Mary Ann's Mud Day by Udry
Mud Tacos by Lopez
The Mud Fairy by Young

More complex Ideas

1. SWIMMING: Of all the recreational sports that children are involved in, not knowing how to swim can mean a life threatening experience. Take your grandchildren to local swim pads if they are available to help them feel comfortable in the water. If there are swim programs in your area, join in. It could save their life! If you are at the beach, swim only in areas with trained lifeguards and read posted signs that tell you about the water conditions.

2. RAIN WALK: Encourage your grandchildren to use all their senses to enjoy a walk in the rain. What happens to the flowers, trees, leaves, animals when it rains? What does the sky look like? How does it feel when the rain drops land on your hand, your face? How does the air smell? Can you see a rainbow? Can you hear the birds? Take off your shoes and walk in the grass, how does it feel? If it is really raining can you channel the water and float some boats?

3. MAKING RAINBOWS: Take a garden hose and spray water up into the air on a sunny day keeping the sun at your back. Can you see the rainbow? What colours can you see? The colours are red, orange, yellow, green, blue, indigo and violet.

4. TOILETS - HOW DO THEY WORK?: The toilet is a place we rarely look but it's fascinating for children. Take the back of the toilet off and let your grandchildren see the way the toilet actually works! An opportunity to discuss low flow toilets. Putting a heavy object in the tank will reduce the amount of water wasted.

5. WATER ORCHESTRA: Fill several glasses with different levels of water and have your grandchildren experiment by tapping to create various sounds.

6. WATER BALLOONS: Water balloons are great fun on a hot day. Make shapes and targets on the wall with chalk and throw your water balloons at them. For a wetter experience toss water balloons back and forth stepping one step back after each successful catch until they break.

7. EARTH DAY: Earth Day is celebrated every year on April 22nd and is a world-wide movement to appreciate and celebrate our planet. Older children might enjoy celebrating Earth Day by creating a T-shirt with their own symbol or logo! White T-shirts for this project can be purchased inexpensively. Markers designed specifi-cally for cloth may enhance this experience. Earth Day is a perfect opportunity to discuss the three Rs – reduce, reuse and recycle!

MY GRAMPA, MADDEN, AGE 4

FUN IN THE SNOW

Simple Ideas

1. SNOW SHOVELS: Don't have enough snow shovels for all your grandchildren? Try using a plastic dust pan – just the right size for little hands.

2. SNOW SNAKE: When you have good packing snow, make snowballs and line them up like a snake. Your grandchildren can decorate the face with items found in nature and they may be interested in spraying the snake with watered down food colouring.

3. SNOW FORT: Build a snow fort by rolling large snowballs for the base and continue until you have a ring. Add as many layers as you can lift. On the outside, pack snow into the holes and don't forget to leave a doorway. Now you are ready to snuggle inside. Add blankets, dishes, pots and pans and have fun!

4. SNOW CASTLES: Create a snow castle by using sand pails and sand toys; provide a variety of other containers for added interest. Add additional props as your grandchildren request them. Old Christmas tree branches can be cut and used for trees.

5. MAPLE TREE CANDY: During the spring if a sugar bush is not available you can take warm maple syrup outside and pour it onto a flat surface of snow. You can place a Popsicle stick into the warm mass and watch it harden into a delicious treat! If you are lucky you might have a maple tree in your own backyard and you can harvest your own syrup.

 FURTHER READING:

From Maple Trees To Maple Syrup by Thoennes Keller
From Seeds To Maple Tree: Following the Life Cycle by Purdie Salas
Maple Trees by Fowler

6. TOUCH WALK: A great opportunity is to go for a feely walk with your grandchild and see which things feel colder – the railing or the wooden door, the tree trunk or an icicle etc. and discuss why.

7. ICY FINGERS: Using disposable gloves, fill them with water and add food colouring. Put them in the freezer and presto you have a frozen hand! When frozen take them outside and place them in a spot where your grandchildren will see them.

8. WINTER CITY: Fill a wide variety of plastic containers, milk cartons, muffin tins with ice and freeze overnight. Add food colouring for extra fun. Remove and let your grandchildren create a city of their own. Add props – wheeled vehicles, little people, wood, material etc!

9. SNOW SPRAY PAINTING: Mix spray bottles with a variety of different food colourings and encourage your grandchildren to paint the snow.

10. FREEZE A SNOWFLAKE: Freeze black paper or black velvet, take it outside and try to catch some snowflakes. Add magnifying glasses to examine each snowflake carefully. Ice crystals join together when falling from the sky to create a snowflake and no two are ever alike.

FURTHER READING:

Millions Of Snowflakes by Siddals
Snowflakes: A Pop Up Book by Preston Chushcoff
Snowflakes And Sparkledust by Thomson

11. WATCH ME MELT: While outside and on a cookie sheet have your grandchildren create their own snowperson and decorate with natural objects, yarn, extra clothing etc. Bring the snowperson inside and watch what happens. Estimate how long it will take for it to melt.

12. LITTLE ICE RINKS: Fill several baking sheets with edges with water. Let freeze. Remove from the tray and your grandchildren now have an ice rink of their own – add "little people", cars, trucks etc.

13. FUNNY WALKS: You and your grandchild could try out a variety of walking styles in the snow – toes in, toes out, one foot in front of another, walk backwards, try sideways, running steps, walking across slippery ice, walking in deep snow, ice skating etc.

FURTHER READING:

Footprints In The Snow by Benjamin
In The Snow: Who's Been Here? By Barrett George

More complex Ideas

1. WINTER SPORT ACTIVITIES: We all need to stay active in winter so what activities would you and your grandchildren enjoy? How about snowboarding, riding on skidoos, ski jumping, cross country skiing, kite skiing, snowshoeing, ice fishing, Polar Bear swimming, curling, hockey, broom ball, tobogganing, ice sailing, luge, dog sledding, skating or speed skating?

2. ICE SKATING: If you have the space and the time to get it ready, nothing is more fun than skating on your own ice rink. Begin by shovelling snow into the area that

you want to use after removing any hazardous materials. You will need to create a snow boarder or use lumber if it is available to keep the water in. Then the stomping begins as your grandchildren tamp down the snow. Wait until the temperature is well below freezing and soak the rink with water over several days. Now you are ready to skate.

 ## FURTHER READING:

The Magic Hockey Stick by Maloney
Z Is For Zamboni: A Hockey Alphabet Book by Napier
Hockey Stars by Shea
I Spy With My Little Eye: Hockey by Napier
The Goalie Mask Hockey Heroes Series by Leonetti

3. SNOW GOLF: Take tuna cans that have been cleaned and embed them in the snow around the backyard. You can make flags and number the "holes". Plastic golf clubs are available or try a second hand sports store and cut the clubs down to your grandchildren's size. Supervise carefully! This works in warmer weather as well!

4. WINTER BOWLING: Fill the bottom of large pop bottles with sand and set them up in a triangle. For bowling balls you can use different size rubber balls depending on your grandchildren's skill level. The bowling "alley" can be as long as you think your grandchildren can manage and mark the end of the alley with food colouring. You may need to stomp down the "alley" for a smoother delivery.

5. TARGET PRACTICE: Use large coffee cans, plastic containers etc. arranged in a pyramid and your grandchildren can throw snowballs to see how many containers they can knock down.

6. SNOW SOCCER: Set up the boundaries for your game and set up a goal at each end. Invite your grandchildren's friends and divide into two teams and play away. Hot chocolate at the end of the game is a good way to celebrate!

7. SNOW BASKETBALL: Have fun making a collection of snowballs and try to see how many snow baskets you can make into a basketball hoop. If you don't have a basketball net try using a garbage can or laundry basket.

8.   WINTER FEEDING: Try placing some peanuts in the snow and the next day observe what has happened. Are there any tracks where you left the peanuts? Let your grandchildren try and decide who visited your backyard overnight. Avoid if peanut allergies are an issue. You might need a field guide to help you discover who has been playing in your yard!

9.   TAKING TEMPERATURES: Try taking temperatures in snow banks. Push the thermometer deep into the snow bank. Ask your grandchildren why they think the temperature is different in some spots?

10. ICE PAINTING: Sprinkle dry tempera paint on paper. Your grandchildren can use ice cubes to blend the dry paint or try an icicle. Ice cubes can be frozen with Popsicle sticks in the centre to make handling the ices more comfortable or use Popsicle makers and use these. If you anticipate that this might be too messy, the same experience can be carried out in an aluminum pie plate or for a larger surface, on a food tray. Add food colouring to the ice cubes for a more complex experience.

11. ICY RACES: Find an area of ice that is flat and conducive to racing cars and trucks along an icy path. Estimate which ones your grandchildren think will travel the farthest. Discuss why this happens or why it doesn't.

12. SNOW HOP SCOTCH: Draw lines for hopscotch in the snow with food colouring and hop away!

13. TIC TAC TOE GAME: Stamp out the frame for the game and play it in the snow. Use two colours of waterproof bean bags as markers.

14. SNOW MAZE: Stamp out a large square or circle shape or be even more creative and create vertical and horizontal lines inside the shape. Play tag with each other but you can't step outside of the rows that have been created.

15. SNOW SHOES: Child size snowshoes are available. Give them a try!

16. WINTER CAMPING: Set up a tent and all the camping gear you can find. Fun for the brave!

17. WINTER PICNIC: Make a winter picnic table out of snow and cover it with a plastic table cloth. Pack up some delicious treats in a picnic basket and enjoy a winter lunch! Eat lots of things to keep you warm – stew, soup, chili, hot chocolate etc.

FURTHER READING:

Earth Day Birthday by Wallace
Fancy Nancy: Every Day Is Earth Day by O'Connor & Preiss Glasser
It's Earth Day by Mayer
Earth Day An Alphabet Book by Kowalski
Earth Day Celebrations In My World by Aloian
Changes by Condon
Keepers Of The Earth: Native Stories And Environmental
Activities For Children by Caduto & Bruchac

"Ice skating was a favourite family activity. I remember hours of skating on our backyard rink that my dad and grandfather made. We skated so long that our toes felt frozen and our feet felt numb. We always had hot chocolate with marshmallows after our skate." DILLON, GRANDSON.

NEIGHBOURHOOD AND THE WORLD

1. TIPS FOR GOING OUT: Depending on the age of your grandchild, if lots of walking is in order, it may be a good idea to bring a stroller. You may be grateful that you brought it. Go early in the day when they are at their best – before naps and lunch, bring along snacks and water and know where the bathrooms are.

2. BE IN THE COMMUNITY: It is important that children have opportunities to explore the world around them - on day trips, on overnight or several day excursions depending on their age. Many children recount these trips as some of their most significant childhood memories. Ideas for visiting in the community might include: aquariums, appliance repair shops, artists' studios, beaches, boat yards, camp grounds, computer shows, construction sites, the court house, ecology trips, factories, farms, forests, government offices, greenhouses, museums, music stores, orchards, playgrounds, theatres, zoos and many more!

3. ON OUR WAY: Take a bus, a subway or a train and go some place new.

4. A BIKE EVENT: Everyone will need a helmet for this adventure along with sunscreen and a water bottle. A safe start is to make sure the bikes are in good working order then ride on designated bike paths. Depending on the skill level of your grandchild you may decide to go either a short or long distance. Make sure your grandchild understands road safety issues and proper hand signals.

5. NEIGHBOURHOOD DETECTIVE: Gardens are everywhere! What's available for walks in your community – parks, nurseries, beaches, open spaces? What can you see, dandelions in sidewalk cracks, buds opening in the spring, cool spaces in the summer because of a canopy of trees, a field of wild flowers, moss growing on rocks, etc. What interesting sculptures have people added to their gardens? Take photos and pick the favourites.

6. MAP IT OUT: Try creating a map of your neighbourhood and see if your grandchildren can plot familiar landmarks, local stores, parks, schools etc.

7. WHAT'S IN GRANNY'S NEIGHBOURHOOD: On a neighbourhood walk check out how different houses have different doors, types of door knobs, paint colours etc. But most importantly where are the playgrounds?

8. THE DOLLAR STORE: Almost every community has a thrift or dollar store and on those days when an adventure is needed, you might give your grandchild a dollar amount which you decide upon before you enter the store. Let your grandchild

choose any object they want. Don't waver about giving more money. This is a practical and important life skill to be learned!

9. STATUES IN THE COMMUNITY: There are many opportunities in our communities to see statues and often they can become the focus of a rich and enlightening discussion.

10. DECORATE THE NEIGHBOURHOOD: Take a wagon for a walk and collect a variety of stones and bring them back home. Use chalk or paint to decorate them, load them back up again and decorate the neighbourhood with the new and beautiful stones!

11. GLOW IN THE DARK CHALK: This is a new and fun idea to try out on your neighbourhood sidewalk!

12. ORGANIZED EVENTS: Go to coffee mornings, parent tot programs, music groups, swimming, baby massage, yoga, and baby gyms. Make use of all the resources in your community.

13. THEATRE, GALLERIES AND THE MOVIES: These venues can be exciting adventures and should be age appropriate. It is important to explain to your grandchild ahead of time what behaviour is expected. Many galleries and museums have programs designated especially for young children. If you can, book your tickets ahead of time so you don't have to wait in long lines.

14. SPORTS EVENTS: We are often invited to attend our grandchildren's sports events! Support your grandchildren whether they win or lose. A great opportunity to role model fair play and good sportsmanship!

15. FESTIVALS AND LOCAL CELEBRATIONS: These festivities are opportunities to connect your grandchildren to the diversity in your community.

16. A CEMETERY VISIT: For older children, much of our local history is "stored" in our cemeteries. There are so many questions that may be relevant to your grandchildren's own personal experiences or the death of a loved animal which may spark questions about death and dying. They may ask why children died so young when they look at death dates on the tomb stones. What famous people might be buried here? Approach with sensitivity and an understanding of your grandchildren ability to manage a difficult topic.

17. VOLUNTEER: Be a volunteer in your grandchild's child care centre or school. Find an organization such as a food bank where you can volunteer together.

18. GO TO WORK: If possible, take your grandchild with you to your work so they can see what you do!

19. LOCAL SHOPS: Start projects that require a trip to a local hardware store, grocery store etc.

20. SPORTS VISIT: Visit the Hockey Hall of Fame or other sports venues of interest.

21. COMPUTER SHOW: This may be an opportunity for your grandchildren to shine and teach you a thing or two while they are at it.

"I have raised two wonderful children, I'm content in my professional and personal life and I get to do a "do-over" with my grandson. But I also know that as I get older I'm a little less resilient. I never used to worry but worry more I do. So trying to keep the worry level low related to my grandson is important so I don't increase his parents worry level." NANCY, GRANDMOTHER

 EATING OUT

Best advice for eating out is – come prepared! Bring all kinds of interesting bits and bobs that will engage and interest your grandchild while you order and wait for your food. You may also want to pick restaurants that are child friendly where you will all feel the most comfortable. You might create a collection of Ziploc bags filled with goodies or a small bag with lots of pockets. Inside you might organize pipe cleaners, origami paper and instruction booklet, stickers, package of interesting markers and paper, books etc. Below there are many ideas that can be taken on a longer trip that could also be brought inside a restaurant. Happy eating and don't forget the wipes!

"My grandparents were really interested in food from a wide range of cultures and we were lucky enough to live in a city with a diverse restaurant scene. They would take us to all kinds of different restaurants that my parents never considered taking us to. We loved the adventure of it all!"
SAM, GRANDSON

ON THE ROAD

If you are starting on a long journey by car or airplane, it is best to come prepared – again! If you are crossing borders you may need a letter signed by your children authorizing the trip as well as giving permission for possible medical care in the case of an emergency. Whether you are off on a long vacation during school holidays or just an overnight trip, consider the age of the children before setting up a travel schedule. Some children travel better than others. It is important to stay as close to their daily routine as possible – naps, meals, bedtimes. Scheduling a car trip when they are ready for their nap may make everyone's life easier. If you are traveling while children are awake, remember, they will need lots of breaks. Car games and activities can provide hours of fun as well as learning. Know when to move on from a game in which they are losing interest. Check out Google maps and look for interesting places stop along the way – plan ahead. Make sure hotels will cater to your needs for a crib or a cot. You may also want to consider destinations where other children will be. Making new friends can be a lifesaver for grandparents!

Trip Essentials:

a. Wipes
b. Change of clothes
c. Diapers
d. Sun hats
e. Sun glasses
f. Water resistant sunscreen (try to keep out of direct sunlight between 11 a.m. and 3 p.m.)

g. Bug spray
h. First aid kit, cough medicine, cream for bug bites, antibiotics for cuts, Band-Aids etc.
i. Backpack to keep you organized

"Seeing things through a child's eyes celebrates the child in you."
DEIRDRE, GRANDMOTHER TO BE

Simple Ideas

1. TRAVEL TREAT BOX: A fishing tackle box at Canadian Tire is perfect with its small sections for storing treats.

2. BOARDS: Try to include clip boards (perfect for clipping papers in place), Etch a Sketch, dry erase boards with a brush and dry erase markers and a magnetic board. A cookie sheet helps to keep crayons etc from falling to the floor and a fold down tray that will fit over the car seat will also provide a firm surface for activities.

3. SEWING PROJECT: For those sitting in the back seat of the car, sew pockets on fabric for items to be stored with a loop over the front seat for easy access to play materials such as markers, pipe cleaners, paper, fancy pens, stickers etc.

4. SPILL PROOF CUPS: Bring these for drinks or for loose items such as Cheerios.

5. SQUEEZY FOODS: Baby foods in pouches are perfect for a no muss no fuss quick and healthy snack. You can also purchase plastic pouches that you can fill with your own healthy smoothies!

6. FOOD: Bring snacks that are easy to open and cause the least amount of mess – fruit strips – foot long are a fun item.

7. SNACK BAGS: Prepare one for each child with their names on them for easy identification. If it's a special occasion, you might wrap all the snacks in festive holiday paper to be opened when they are hungry.

8. GOODIE BAG: Take a trip to the dollar store and wrap gifts that can be opened throughout the trip to create some suspense.

9. THEIR INTEREST BAG: You can use a simple drawstring bag and put in items of particular interest to your grandchild, for example a bag full of dinosaurs and a cookie sheet will provide hours of fun!

10. USBORNE: Usborne has created a wonderful set of wipe clean activity cards with a pen called *100 Things For Little Children To Do On A Journey*. There are matching games, puzzles to solve, pictures to draw and things to spot. Because they are wipe-clean they can be used over and over again.

11. BOOKS: Bring along special books for them to read or for you to read to them. If you are the reader, choose a book with terrific pictures to ensure their interest. Bring books that may be about your destination.

12. STORYTELLING: Be prepared to make up incredible stories to help the time pass. Another idea is that each person adds a new sentence to a new story.

13. DVDS: Some cars come equipped with DVD players and may be just the thing for a tired and cranky child. There are also portable DVD players on the market that can be used both at your home or on the road.

14. AUDIO BOOKS: You can get audio books on tape at the local library

15. MAGAZINES: Magazines will be a welcome addition about half way through your road trip.

16. COLORFORMS: These plastic shapes can be put on the car window and arranged several times over.

17. STENCILS: Coloured pencils and stencils can help while away the hours.

18. MUSIC: Theirs and yours - play classical music for cool down. Draw to the music. Learn the songs the children are singing, most words are available on line so you may want to print out the words before you leave. Sing your favourite tunes as well. Create a playlist for both before you leave.

19. NAME THAT TUNE: Pause your playlist and see if they can name the song.

20. WINDOW MARKERS: These markers can be wiped clean with a moistened towelette.

21. DOT TO DOT: There are online dot games you can print off ahead of time.

22. STICKERS: Nothing is more fun than a new pack of stickers. Place a paper on a clip board and the children can peel away.

23. PAPER DOLLS: Hours may pass if your grandchild is interested in cutting out clothes for their paper dolls.

24. DISPOSABLE CAMERA: A disposable camera to record their own trip can be great fun for little hands and you don't have to worry about damage to a really good camera.

"I hate to admit it but I am the grandmother who takes out a photo album full of my most recent shots of my grandson whenever I meet up with my friends! He's so beautiful; I just can't help but share in the fun!" FATIMA, JADDA

25. MAGNIFYING GLASS: This is a fun addition to any car ride.

26. SEWING CARDS: You can make simple sewing cards by drawing your child's favourite animal, car or object on heavy duty cardstock then punching holes around the edges. You can use bodkin needles and yarn for sewing or put the end of your yarn into some white glue and let it dry and it will be strong enough to allow your grandchild to push the yarn through the holes. You can also use a shoelace!

27. POST CARDS: If your grandchild is feeling homesick, stopping to send a postcard home to their parents may do the trick. Save post cards on your travels and make a reminder book when you get home.

28. NIGHT DRIVING: Bring flashlights, glow sticks, bracelets and/or necklaces for night driving.

29. LEGO: Use a lunch box with a secure lock and bring along Lego for older children and Duplo for younger ones.

30. PLAY A GAME: Fortunately, unfortunately – Unfortunately there is an alligator in the car, fortunately he only eats bananas etc.

31. I SPY: An age old favourite!

32. BINGO/EYE SPY: You can draw objects on a sheet of paper and laminate them so that your grandchildren can use wipe off markers when they spot the object or you can create a grid on your computer like a bingo card and use clip art to download things the children might see on this particular journey. For little ones pick objects that are easily found – truck, scooter, bus and more challenging ones for older children – red car, horse, plane etc.

33. A TO Z: Look out the window and each person tries to find something that begins with letter A. When something is found, everyone is on to the next letter – B.

34. GUESSING GAME/20 QUESTIONS: Everyone gets 20 questions to try and guess who I am?

35. LICENSE PLATE GAME: How many provinces, states etc. can you find?

36. COLOUR GAME: Spot a car in a certain colour, for example, if it's red yell fire.

37. TUNNEL: An old family tradition! When going through a tunnel see if you can hold your breath until you are out the other side.

38. GARBAGE: Decorate brown paper bags to use as car litter bags.

39. BUBBLES: When you come to a car stop for washrooms and food, find a safe place and bring out the bubbles. Your grandchildren will run about trying to catch the bubbles and it will help them run off all that energy.

40. ROAD STOPS: Bring along a ball and some gloves, older children might appreciate an opportunity to play catch at a road stop. Other ideas might be jump ropes, toss a Frisbee about or throw a football.

41. KEEP SAKES: Keep a rock jar with a rock from every trip. Paint the favourites.

More complex Ideas

1. PORTA PAKS: You can make these before your road trip and slip games and puzzlers into Ziploc bags. Examples: #1 Lay tongue depressors out on the table and cover them with glue. Lay a picture of your grandchild on top of the tongue depressors, press in place and let dry. With an exacto knife, slice between the tongue depressors and now you have a personalized puzzle. #2 Cut up the front of a cereal box into pieces, cut up their drawings (with their permission), cut up a family photo or an old calendar or postcard and presto you have another puzzle.

2. GAME BINDER: You can create your own paper and marker games with clear plastic sleeves and a wipe off marker with a game inside and wipe off when done. Punch with a three hole punch and load up the game binder.

3. DIRECTIONS: Give the kids the map.

4. MAD LIBS FOR KIDS: Print these fun things off for the car ride at:

@ www.classroomjr.com/printable-mad-libs-for-kids/

5. JOURNAL: Create a trip diary with fancy markers.

6. ROAD TRIP QUESTIONNAIRE: You can make up all kinds of quizzes such as a quiz all about your grandchild - favourite colour, food etc. or a quiz about where you are going and what you might see there.

7. ALLOWANCE: Give them an "allowance" each day. This prevents many requests for money to buy treats they see along the way. Once the agreed upon amount is gone – it's gone!

8. STRING GAMES: String games increase children's creativity and dexterity. All you need is string! There are many books with interesting ideas to do with string games.

 FURTHER READING:

Cat's Cradle, Owl's Eyes: A Book Of String Games by Gryski
Many Stars And More String Games by Gryski

Pull The Other One: String Games And Stories by Taylor
String Games by Darsie

9. REMEMBER GAME: We All Went Shopping and I Bought... or I'm Going on a Picnic. Each person must remember every item that was said before their turn then add an item of their own.

10. PAPER GAMES: Hangman, X and Os.

11. PICTIONARY: Draw and guess.

12. ELECTRONIC DEVICES: You may want to include their electronic devices to help pass the time. If it is a long trip you may want to monitor their use.

13. CAMERA: Older children may be able to manage a more expensive camera or their cell phone. Help your grandchildren sequence the photos they took on your trip and put them in a scrap book.

14. BRAIN TEASERS: Brain Quest cards, Trivial Pursuit cards, Sudoku for kids are now available.

"I see myself, my parents, her grandmother, her aunt in my granddaughter. She is a mosaic of those who came before, holding our hopes in her little hands." TERRY, GRAMPA

 FURTHER READING:

Hard Nuts Of History Ultimate Quiz and Game Book by Turner
National Geographic Kids Quiz Whiz 5: 1,000 Super Fun Mind-bending
Totally Awesome Trivia Questions by National Geographic Kids

@ ONLINE IDEAS:

www.pitara.com/category/quizzes-for-kids/history-quizzes-for-kids/

www.squiglysplayhouse.com/Games/Quizzes/Animals/AnimalGiants

www.funtrivia.com/

www.kidsmathgamesonline.com/quizzes

ca.ixl.com/math/jr-kindergarten/identify-circles-squares-and-triangles

ONE LAST THOUGHT!

It is my hope that the ideas in this book have helped you form a special bond between you and your grandchild. Each person brings their own unique approach to the role of a grandparent. Whether you see yourself as a role model, a mentor, a nurturer, historian, chauffeur, or buddy, never underestimate the influence you have in the lives of your grandchildren. There can never be enough caring adults in a child's life! How lucky are we to have our grandchildren in our lives! They bring love, sparkle and incredible enthusiasm to our relationships. Savour it, honour it!

ICONS AND THE ARTIST —
NOUN PROJECT

CPSIA information can be obtained
at www.ICGtesting.com
Printed in the USA
BVHW020254230821
614888BV00002B/19